Mastering

EXPONENTIAL

MOVING AVERAGES

by

Lalit Mohanty

PREFACE

Welcome to "Mastering Exponential Moving Averages: A Comprehensive Guide to Trading Success." In the fast-paced world of financial markets, success often hinges on one's ability to interpret and act upon market signals swiftly and accurately. Among the myriad of tools available to traders, exponential moving averages (EMAs) stand out as versatile and powerful instruments for technical analysis.

This book is a culmination of years of experience, research, and real-world application of EMAs in trading. Whether you're a seasoned professional seeking to refine your strategies or a newcomer eager to delve into the world of technical analysis, this guide is designed to provide you with the knowledge and tools necessary to leverage EMAs effectively in your trading journey.

Within these pages, you'll embark on a comprehensive exploration of EMAs, from their historical roots to advanced trading strategies. We'll unravel the mathematical intricacies behind EMAs, examine their role in identifying trends and reversals, and delve into practical techniques for incorporating them into your trading arsenal.

Table of Contents

Chapter 1: Introduction to Exponential Moving Averages (EMAs)

- Understanding the basics of moving averages

- Introducing the concept of exponential smoothing

- Differentiating between simple moving averages and exponential moving averages

Chapter 2: Historical Perspective of Moving Averages in Trading

- Tracing the evolution of moving averages in financial markets

- Examining the role of EMAs in technical analysis

- Highlighting key milestones and breakthroughs

Chapter 3: The Mathematics Behind Exponential Moving Averages

- Delving into the formula and calculations of EMAs

- Explaining the significance of weighting factors

- Illustrating how EMAs respond to recent price action

Chapter 4: Setting the Foundation: Choosing the Right Timeframes

- Selecting appropriate time periods for short-term and long-term analysis

- Understanding the impact of timeframes on trading signals

Chapter 10: Fine-Tuning Entries and Exits

- Refining entry points using EMAs

- Timing exits based on EMA crossovers and price action

- Implementing trailing stops for optimal risk management

Chapter 11: Multi-Timeframe Analysis with EMAs

- Leveraging EMAs across different timeframes

- Enhancing overall trend analysis with multi-timeframe strategies

- Avoiding common pitfalls in multi-timeframe analysis

Chapter 12: EMA Strategies for Day Trading

- Adapting EMAs for intraday trading

- Developing intraday strategies with EMAs

- Addressing challenges specific to day trading

Chapter 13: Swing Trading Strategies with EMAs

- Customizing EMAs for swing trading

- Identifying optimal swing trading setups

- Managing swing trades effectively with EMAs

Chapter 14: Backtesting and Optimization

- The importance of backtesting in EMA-based strategies

- Practical tips for effective backtesting

- Optimizing EMA parameters for maximum performance

Chapter 15: Psychological Aspects of Trading with EMAs

- Understanding the emotional impact of EMA signals

- Managing psychological challenges during drawdowns

- Building discipline and resilience in EMA-based trading

Chapter 16: Automation and Algorithmic Trading with EMAs

- Exploring algorithmic trading strategies with EMAs

- Implementing EMA-based trading bots

- Balancing automation with human discretion

Chapter 17: Common Mistakes and Pitfalls

- Identifying and avoiding common EMA-related mistakes

- Learning from the experiences of unsuccessful traders

- Strategies for overcoming challenges and setbacks

Chapter 18: Case Studies of Successful EMA Traders

- Profiling successful traders who rely on EMAs

- Analyzing their strategies and decision-making processes

- Extracting valuable lessons from real-world examples

Chapter 19: Adapting to Changing Market Conditions

- Recognizing shifts in market dynamics

- Adjusting EMA strategies to volatile and ranging markets

- Staying agile in response to economic and geopolitical events

Chapter 20: Incorporating Fundamental Analysis with EMAs

- Integrating fundamental factors into EMA-based trading

- Balancing technical and fundamental analysis

- Case studies of successful traders combining both approaches

Chapter 21: Custom EMA Indicators and Tools

- Creating custom EMA indicators

- Exploring third-party tools for advanced EMA analysis

- Enhancing the toolkit for EMA traders

Chapter 22: Alternative Uses of EMAs

- Utilizing EMAs for sentiment analysis

- Applying EMAs to cryptocurrency and forex markets

- Innovations and creative uses of EMAs in trading

Chapter 23: Trading Psychology and Discipline

- The role of discipline in successful trading

- Developing a resilient mindset with EMAs

- Strategies for overcoming common psychological challenges

Chapter 24: Regulatory and Ethical Considerations

- Navigating regulatory challenges in EMA-based trading

- Ethical considerations in using technical indicators

- Promoting responsible and transparent trading practices

Chapter 25: Combining EMAs with Other Technical Indicators

- Enhancing analysis by integrating EMAs with oscillators

- Exploring synergy with other popular indicators

- Avoiding conflicting signals through effective combinations

Chapter 26: EMA Strategies for Different Assets

- Tailoring EMA strategies to specific asset classes

- Strategies for stocks, commodities, and currencies

- Addressing unique challenges in each market

Chapter 27: Continuous Learning and Adaptation

- The importance of ongoing education in trading

- Staying updated on EMA-related developments

- Adapting strategies to evolving market conditions

Chapter 28: Social Trading and Community Involvement

- Leveraging social platforms for EMA trading insights

- Joining communities of EMA traders

- Collaborating and learning from peers in the field

Chapter 29: Building a Personalized EMA Trading System

- Creating a unique EMA-based trading system

- Tailoring strategies to individual risk tolerance and goals

- Documenting and refining the personalized system over time

Chapter 30: Risk Management Strategies with EMAs

- Implementing effective risk management techniques

- Calculating position sizes based on EMA signals

- Strategies for preserving capital during adverse market conditions

Chapter 31: The Future of EMAs in Trading

- Emerging trends in EMA-based trading strategies

- Technological advancements shaping the future of EMAs

- Predictions for the role of EMAs in financial markets

Chapter 32: Realizing Success: Stories from EMA Traders

- Compiling success stories from traders who mastered EMAs

- Lessons learned from their journeys to profitability

- Inspiring and motivating aspiring EMA traders

Chapter 33: Conclusion and Actionable Insights

- Summarizing key takeaways from the book

- Providing actionable insights for immediate implementation

- Encouraging continuous growth and improvement in EMA-based trading

CHAPTER 1

INTRODUCTION TO EXPONENTIAL MOVING AVERAGES (EMAS)

In the realm of technical analysis, moving averages serve as foundational tools for traders seeking to interpret and anticipate market trends. Among the various types of moving averages, the exponential moving average (EMA) stands out for its ability to provide a more responsive and nuanced representation of price data. This chapter serves as a primer on EMAs, offering insights into their fundamental principles and distinguishing features.

Understanding the Basics of Moving Averages

Moving averages, in essence, are mathematical calculations that smooth out price data over a specified period, revealing underlying trends by filtering out short-term fluctuations. They are widely used by traders and analysts to identify trend direction, gauge market momentum, and spot potential reversal points.

The simplest form of moving average is the **simple moving average (SMA)**, which calculates the average price of an asset over a predetermined number of periods. For instance, a 50-day SMA computes the average closing price of the asset over the last 50 days. While SMAs offer a straightforward way to analyze trends, they suffer from a drawback: equal weighting is assigned to each data point in the calculation, potentially causing lagging responses to recent price movements.

Introducing the Concept of Exponential Smoothing

To address the limitations of SMAs, exponential moving averages employ a more dynamic calculation method known as exponential smoothing. Unlike SMAs, where all data points carry equal weight, EMAs assign greater significance to recent price data, resulting in a more responsive indicator.

The formula for calculating an EMA involves applying a smoothing factor (alpha) to the previous period's EMA value and adding a proportion of the current period's price. This exponentially decreasing weighting scheme ensures that recent price movements exert a more pronounced influence on the EMA, leading to quicker adjustments to changing market conditions.

Differentiating Between Simple Moving Averages and Exponential Moving Averages

While both SMAs and EMAs serve similar purposes in trend analysis, they exhibit distinct characteristics that make them suitable for different trading scenarios. SMAs are preferred for their simplicity and stability, making them well-suited for identifying long-term trends and major support/resistance levels.

On the other hand, EMAs excel in capturing short-term price fluctuations and reacting promptly to market reversals. Their responsiveness to recent price changes makes them invaluable for traders seeking to capitalize on momentum shifts and identify entry and exit points with greater precision.

In summary, while SMAs offer reliability and robustness over longer periods, EMAs provide enhanced sensitivity to recent price action, making them indispensable tools for active traders navigating dynamic market conditions.

As we delve deeper into the realm of EMAs in the subsequent chapters, we'll explore how to harness their power effectively, develop comprehensive trading strategies, and unlock the full potential of technical analysis in achieving trading success.

CHAPTER 2

HISTORICAL PERSPECTIVE OF MOVING AVERAGES IN TRADING

Moving averages, including the exponential moving average (EMA), have played a pivotal role in the evolution of technical analysis within financial markets. This chapter delves into the historical context of moving averages, tracing their journey from early developments to their current prominence in trading strategies.

Tracing the Evolution of Moving Averages in Financial Markets

The use of moving averages traces back to the early 20th century when technical analysis began gaining traction among traders and investors. At its inception, moving averages were calculated manually, requiring extensive computations and charting efforts. Despite these challenges, traders recognized the value of moving averages in smoothing price data and identifying underlying trends.

Over the decades, advancements in computing technology facilitated the widespread adoption of moving averages, enabling traders to analyze larger datasets and refine their trading strategies. Moving averages became indispensable tools for trend identification, providing traders with valuable insights into market dynamics and potential entry/exit points.

Examining the Role of EMAs in Technical Analysis

As technical analysis methodologies evolved, so did the sophistication of moving average calculations. The introduction of exponential smoothing techniques marked a significant breakthrough in moving average analysis, giving rise to exponential moving averages (EMAs). Unlike their simpler counterparts, EMAs offered greater responsiveness to recent price movements, allowing traders to adapt more swiftly to changing market conditions.

EMAs quickly gained popularity among traders seeking to capitalize on short-term trends and momentum shifts. Their ability to reflect current market sentiment with precision made them invaluable tools for active traders navigating volatile markets. Today, EMAs are widely incorporated into various technical analysis frameworks, serving as key indicators in trend-following and reversal strategies.

Highlighting Key Milestones and Breakthroughs

Throughout history, several milestones have shaped the evolution of moving averages and their application in trading:

1. **Development of Exponential Smoothing Techniques**: The pioneering work of mathematicians and statisticians in refining exponential smoothing methods laid the foundation for the creation of EMAs.

2. **Introduction of Computerized Trading Platforms**: The advent of electronic trading platforms revolutionized the accessibility and efficiency of moving average analysis,

enabling traders to execute strategies with unprecedented speed and accuracy.

3. **Integration of EMAs in Algorithmic Trading**: The rise of algorithmic trading brought about a new era of automated strategies, with EMAs serving as key components in many algorithmic trading systems.

4. **Advancements in Data Analytics**: Innovations in data analytics and machine learning have further enhanced the capabilities of moving average analysis, enabling traders to extract deeper insights from market data and develop more sophisticated trading strategies.

By understanding the historical context and evolution of moving averages, traders can appreciate the significance of these indicators in modern financial markets. As we delve deeper into the practical applications of EMAs in the subsequent chapters, we'll explore how traders can leverage these powerful tools to navigate the complexities of today's trading landscape and achieve their financial goals.

CHAPTER 3

THE MATHEMATICS BEHIND EXPONENTIAL MOVING AVERAGES

Exponential Moving Averages (EMAs) are a foundational tool in technical analysis, renowned for their responsiveness to recent price action. In this chapter, we'll delve into the mathematical underpinnings of EMAs, unraveling the formulae and calculations behind these dynamic indicators. We'll also explore the significance of weighting factors and illustrate how EMAs respond to changes in market conditions.

Understanding the Formula and Calculations of EMAs

The formula for calculating an EMA involves a multi-step process that emphasizes recent price data while still incorporating historical prices. Let's break down the steps:

1. **Calculate the SMA**: Begin by computing the Simple Moving Average (SMA) over a specified period, typically denoted as N.

This involves summing up the closing prices of the asset over the past N periods and dividing by N.

2. **Calculate the Smoothing Factor**: The smoothing factor, denoted as α, determines the weight given to the most recent price data. It is calculated using the formula $\alpha=2/N+1$, where N is the number of periods.

3. **Calculate the EMA**: Once the SMA is obtained, calculate the EMA for the current period using the formula:

$$EMA_t = (Close_t - EMA_{t-1}) \times \alpha + EMA_{t-1}$$

Where:

EMA_t is for the current period t

$Close_t$ is the closing price for the current period,

$EMAt-1$ is the EMA for the previous period,

α is the smoothing factor

Explaining the Significance of Weighting Factors

The smoothing factor, α, plays a crucial role in determining the responsiveness of the EMA to recent price changes. A smaller value of α assigns greater weight to historical data, resulting in a smoother and less reactive EMA. Conversely, a larger value of α places more emphasis on recent prices, making the EMA more sensitive to short-term fluctuations.

By adjusting the smoothing factor, traders can tailor the EMA to suit their specific trading preferences and market conditions. Shorter periods with higher α values are favored for capturing rapid price movements, while longer periods with lower α values provide a broader perspective on trend direction.

Illustrating How EMAs Respond to Recent Price Action

EMAs are renowned for their ability to respond swiftly to changes in market sentiment, thanks to their exponential weighting scheme. Unlike Simple Moving Averages, which offer equal weight to all data points, EMAs assign progressively decreasing weights to older data, prioritizing recent price action.

As a result, EMAs exhibit greater responsiveness to recent price movements, enabling traders to identify emerging trends and potential reversal points with precision. This responsiveness is particularly advantageous in fast-paced markets, where timely decision-making is critical for success.

In summary, the mathematics behind EMAs underscore their versatility and effectiveness as tools for technical analysis. By understanding the formulae, significance of weighting factors, and response mechanisms of EMAs, traders can harness the full potential of these dynamic indicators to inform their trading decisions and achieve their financial objectives.

CHAPTER 4

SETTING THE FOUNDATION: CHOOSING THE RIGHT TIMEFRAMES

Selecting the appropriate timeframe is a crucial aspect of using Exponential Moving Averages (EMAs) effectively in trading. In this chapter, we'll explore the significance of choosing the right time periods for short-term and long-term analysis. We'll also discuss how different timeframes impact trading signals and strategies, along with techniques for fine-tuning EMAs to match prevailing market conditions.

Selecting Appropriate Time Periods for Short-term and Long-term Analysis

The choice of timeframe greatly influences the interpretation of EMA signals and the suitability of trading strategies. Short-term traders typically focus on shorter timeframes, such as intraday or daily charts, to capture rapid price movements and capitalize on short-term trends. Conversely, long-term investors may opt for longer timeframes, such as weekly or monthly charts, to identify broader market trends and investment opportunities.

When selecting time periods for EMAs, consider the trading style, objectives, and risk tolerance:

- **Short-term Analysis**: For short-term trading, consider using shorter EMAs, such as 5-day or 10-day EMAs, to capture rapid price changes and intraday trends.

- **Long-term Analysis**: For long-term investing or swing trading, longer EMAs, such as 50-day or 200-day EMAs, provide a broader perspective on trend direction and help filter out short-term noise.

Understanding the Impact of Timeframes on Trading Signals

The timeframe chosen for EMAs influences the signals generated and the reliability of those signals. Shorter EMAs produce more frequent signals but are prone to false signals and whipsaws, especially in choppy or range-bound markets. Longer EMAs, on the other hand, generate fewer signals but offer greater reliability, particularly in trending markets.

Traders should be mindful of the trade-offs associated with different timeframes:

- **Shorter Timeframes**: Offer more opportunities for active trading but require closer monitoring and may result in more transaction costs.

- **Longer Timeframes**: Provide clearer trend signals and require less frequent adjustments but may lead to missed opportunities in rapidly changing markets.

Fine-tuning EMAs to Match Market Conditions

Adapting EMAs to match prevailing market conditions is essential for optimizing trading strategies. In volatile markets, shorter EMAs are more responsive and better suited for capturing rapid price movements. Conversely, in stable or range-bound markets, longer EMAs provide smoother signals and help filter out noise.

Traders can fine-tune EMAs based on market volatility and price dynamics:

- **High Volatility**: Use shorter EMAs to capture short-term trends and react quickly to market changes.

- **Low Volatility**: Employ longer EMAs to reduce noise and generate more reliable signals in choppy markets.

By adjusting the parameters of EMAs to align with current market conditions, traders can enhance the effectiveness of their trading strategies and improve the accuracy of their trade decisions.

In summary, selecting the right timeframes for EMAs is a foundational step in building successful trading strategies. Whether trading short-term momentum or long-term trends, understanding the impact of timeframes on trading signals and fine-tuning EMAs to match market conditions are key principles for achieving consistent profitability in the financial markets.

CHAPTER 5

TYPES OF EXPONENTIAL MOVING AVERAGES

Exponential Moving Averages (EMAs) come in various configurations, each offering unique advantages and drawbacks. In this chapter, we'll explore the different types of EMAs, including single, double, and triple EMAs. We'll analyze the strengths and weaknesses of each type and provide practical applications to help traders effectively incorporate them into their trading strategies.

Exploring Single, Double, and Triple EMAs

1. **Single EMA**: A single EMA is the most basic form of exponential moving average, calculated using a single smoothing factor. It gives more weight to recent price data, making it highly responsive to short-term price movements.

2. **Double EMA**: The double EMA, also known as the double exponential moving average (DEMA), applies exponential smoothing twice to the price series. This amplifies the

responsiveness to recent price changes, resulting in even faster adjustments to market conditions.

3. **Triple EMA**: The triple EMA, or triple exponential moving average (TEMA), further enhances responsiveness by applying exponential smoothing three times. This heightened sensitivity to recent price action minimizes lag and provides exceptionally accurate signals in fast-moving markets.

Analyzing the Strengths and Weaknesses of Each Type

- **Single EMA**: Strengths include its simplicity and responsiveness to short-term trends. However, it can be prone to false signals in choppy or range-bound markets due to its high sensitivity to price fluctuations.

- **Double EMA**: The double EMA offers enhanced responsiveness and reduced lag compared to single EMAs, making it effective for capturing rapid price movements. Its drawback lies in increased noise, which can lead to more frequent false signals.

- **Triple EMA**: TEMA excels in filtering out noise and providing accurate signals in volatile markets. Its main weakness is the complexity of calculation, which may deter some traders. Additionally, it may generate fewer signals compared to single or double EMAs.

Practical Applications of Different EMA Configurations

- **Single EMA**: Useful for short-term traders looking to capitalize on intraday trends or momentum bursts. It can be applied in conjunction with other indicators to confirm signals and filter out false positives.

- **Double EMA**: Ideal for traders seeking faster responses to market changes without sacrificing too much reliability. It's commonly used in trend-following strategies to capture strong trends while avoiding whipsaws.

- **Triple EMA**: Suited for traders who prioritize accuracy and are willing to tolerate slightly fewer trading signals. TEMA is particularly effective in volatile markets, where precise timing is crucial for successful trading.

By understanding the strengths and weaknesses of each type of EMA and their practical applications, traders can tailor their strategies to match their trading objectives and prevailing market conditions. Experimenting with different EMA configurations and combining them with other technical indicators can help traders develop robust and adaptable trading approaches that yield consistent results.

CHAPTER 6

BUILDING A SOLID TRADING STRATEGY WITH EMAS

Exponential Moving Averages (EMAs) are powerful tools in the trader's arsenal, but using them effectively requires a comprehensive trading strategy. In this chapter, we'll discuss how to integrate EMAs into a cohesive trading plan, combine them with other technical indicators, and establish risk management parameters to safeguard your capital.

Integrating EMAs into a Comprehensive Trading Plan

1. **Define Trading Objectives**: Begin by clarifying your trading goals, whether it's short-term profit maximization, long-term wealth accumulation, or risk mitigation.

2. **Select Suitable Timeframes**: Choose appropriate EMA periods based on your trading style and objectives. Short-term traders may opt for shorter EMAs, while long-term investors may prefer longer EMAs for trend identification.

3. **Identify Entry and Exit Signals**: Determine the criteria for entering and exiting trades based on EMA crossovers, trend strength, and market conditions.

4. **Set Position Sizing Rules**: Establish guidelines for position sizing based on risk tolerance, account size, and market volatility.

Combining EMAs with Other Technical Indicators

1. **Trend Confirmation with Oscillators**: Use oscillators such as the Relative Strength Index (RSI) or Stochastic Oscillator to confirm EMA signals and avoid false positives.

2. **Volume Analysis**: Incorporate volume analysis to validate EMA signals. High volume during EMA crossovers enhances their reliability, signaling strong market participation.

3. **Support and Resistance Levels**: Identify key support and resistance levels using price action analysis. EMA bounces off these levels can serve as additional confirmation for trade entries and exits.

4. **Additional Trend Indicators**: Consider using complementary trend indicators such as Moving Average Convergence Divergence (MACD) or Ichimoku Cloud to reinforce EMA signals and provide additional insights into market trends.

Establishing Risk Management Parameters

1. **Determine Stop-loss Levels**: Set stop-loss orders based on technical levels, volatility, and risk-reward ratios. Adjust stop-loss levels dynamically as the trade progresses to protect profits and limit losses.

2. **Implement Position Sizing Rules**: Calculate position sizes based on risk per trade, account size, and stop-loss distance.

Avoid over-leveraging by adhering to predetermined risk limits.

3. **Monitor Portfolio Exposure**: Maintain a diversified portfolio to reduce concentration risk. Limit exposure to individual assets or sectors to mitigate the impact of adverse market movements.

4. **Review and Adjust Risk Parameters**: Regularly review and adjust risk management parameters based on changing market conditions, performance evaluation, and evolving trading objectives.

By integrating EMAs into a comprehensive trading plan, combining them with other technical indicators, and establishing robust risk management parameters, traders can build a solid foundation for success in the financial markets. Consistency, discipline, and adaptability are key principles in implementing an effective trading strategy with EMAs, helping traders navigate the complexities of market dynamics and achieve their financial goals.

CHAPTER 7

IDENTIFYING TREND REVERSALS WITH EMAS

Trend reversals represent critical junctures in financial markets, offering opportunities for traders to capitalize on shifts in market sentiment. In this chapter, we'll explore how Exponential Moving Averages (EMAs) can be utilized to identify signals of trend exhaustion and potential reversals. We'll delve into practical techniques for recognizing reversal patterns and provide real-world examples of successful trades facilitated by EMAs.

Recognizing Signals of Trend Exhaustion

1. **Divergence**: Look for divergences between price and EMA indicators, where the price moves in one direction while the EMAs move in the opposite direction. Bearish divergence occurs when prices make higher highs while EMAs make lower highs, signaling weakening bullish momentum, and vice versa for bullish divergence.

2. **Overbought/Oversold Conditions**: Monitor EMA-based oscillators such as the Moving Average Convergence Divergence (MACD) or Relative Strength Index (RSI) for overbought or oversold conditions. Extreme readings suggest the potential exhaustion of the prevailing trend and a possible reversal.

3. **Candlestick Patterns**: Pay attention to reversal candlestick patterns such as Doji, Hammer, Shooting Star, and Engulfing patterns occurring near EMA levels. These patterns often indicate indecision in the market and can precede trend reversals.

Utilizing EMAs to Identify Potential Trend Reversals

1. **EMA Crossovers**: Watch for EMA crossovers, where a shorter-term EMA crosses above or below a longer-term EMA. A bearish crossover (shorter-term EMA crossing below longer-term EMA) suggests a potential downtrend reversal, while a bullish crossover (shorter-term EMA crossing above longer-term EMA) indicates a potential uptrend reversal.

2. **Price-EMA Confluence**: Identify key EMA levels that coincide with significant support or resistance levels on the price chart. Reversal signals near these confluence zones carry greater significance and provide higher-probability trade setups.

3. **Confirmation from Volume**: Confirm potential reversal signals with changes in trading volume. An increase in volume accompanying a reversal signal strengthens the validity of the reversal pattern.

Real-world Examples of Successful Reversal Trades

1. **Bearish Reversal Trade**: A bearish divergence between the price and a shorter-term EMA (e.g., 10-day EMA) occurs after a

prolonged uptrend. A bearish crossover between the 10-day and 50-day EMAs confirms the reversal signal. Traders enter short positions as the price breaks below key support levels, targeting the next support area.

2. **Bullish Reversal Trade**: A bullish engulfing candlestick pattern forms near the 200-day EMA after a prolonged downtrend. The bullish engulfing pattern, accompanied by a bullish crossover between shorter-term EMAs, signals a potential trend reversal. Traders enter long positions with a stop-loss below the recent swing low, targeting resistance levels.

Conclusion

Identifying trend reversals with EMAs requires a combination of technical analysis techniques and a keen understanding of market dynamics. By recognizing signals of trend exhaustion, utilizing EMAs to identify potential reversals, and leveraging real-world examples, traders can enhance their ability to capitalize on trend reversals and navigate market transitions with confidence. However, it's essential to exercise caution and implement risk management measures to mitigate potential losses in volatile trading environments.

CHAPTER 8

RIDING THE TREND: TREND FOLLOWING WITH EMAS

Trend following strategies are among the most popular approaches in trading, allowing traders to profit from sustained price movements. In this chapter, we'll explore how Exponential Moving Averages (EMAs) can be utilized to develop robust trend following strategies. We'll discuss techniques for identifying strong trends, recognizing trend continuation signals with EMAs, and managing positions during trending markets.

Developing Strategies to Ride Strong Trends

1. **Trend Identification**: Begin by identifying the prevailing trend using EMAs. A bullish trend is characterized by prices consistently trading above key EMAs (e.g., 50-day and 200-day EMAs), while a bearish trend is indicated by prices trading below these EMAs.

2. **Entry Timing**: Wait for pullbacks or retracements within the trend to enter positions. Look for areas where the price touches or bounces off key EMAs, signaling potential entry points in the direction of the trend.

3. **Risk Management**: Set stop-loss orders below swing lows in uptrends or above swing highs in downtrends to protect against adverse price movements. Adjust position sizes based on volatility and risk tolerance to manage downside risk.

Identifying Trend Continuation Signals with EMAs

1. **EMA Crossovers**: Utilize EMA crossovers to identify trend continuation signals. In an uptrend, look for bullish crossovers where shorter-term EMAs cross above longer-term EMAs. Conversely, in a downtrend, watch for bearish crossovers where shorter-term EMAs cross below longer-term EMAs.

2. **Trend Strength**: Monitor the slope and spacing between EMAs to gauge the strength of the trend. Steeper slopes and wider separations between EMAs indicate stronger trends, while flattening slopes and narrowing separations suggest weakening momentum.

3. **Volume Confirmation**: Confirm trend continuation signals with changes in trading volume. Increasing volume during EMA crossovers or trend pullbacks reinforces the validity of the trend continuation pattern.

Managing Positions During Trending Markets

1. **Trail Stop-losses**: Adjust stop-loss orders dynamically to lock in profits as the trend progresses. Trail stop-losses below (in uptrends) or above (in downtrends) key EMAs or swing lows/highs to capture gains while allowing for potential trend extensions.

2. **Pyramiding Positions**: Consider adding to winning positions as the trend unfolds, commonly known as pyramiding. Scale into trades by adding to positions on pullbacks or breakouts, using EMAs as reference points for entry.

3. **Take Profits Gradually**: Gradually scale out of positions as the trend matures to realize profits. Consider scaling out of positions at predetermined target levels or when signs of trend exhaustion emerge, such as divergences or overbought/oversold conditions.

Conclusion

Riding the trend with EMAs involves patience, discipline, and a keen understanding of market dynamics. By developing strategies to identify strong trends, recognizing trend continuation signals with EMAs, and effectively managing positions during trending markets, traders can capitalize on profitable trend-following opportunities. However, it's essential to remain adaptable and adjust strategies based on evolving market conditions to navigate trend reversals and mitigate potential losses.

CHAPTER 9

THE GOLDEN CROSS AND DEATH CROSS PHENOMENA

The Golden Cross and Death Cross are two widely recognized technical patterns that hold significant implications for traders and investors. In this chapter, we'll delve into the intricacies of these phenomena, exploring their significance, implications, and real-world examples that demonstrate their reliability as trading signals.

Understanding the Significance of the Golden Cross

The Golden Cross occurs when a shorter-term Exponential Moving Average (EMA), typically the 50-day EMA, crosses above a longer-term EMA, such as the 200-day EMA. This bullish crossover signals a potential shift from a downtrend to an uptrend, often regarded as a bullish reversal pattern.

Implications of the Golden Cross:

1. **Confirmation of Trend Reversal**: The Golden Cross confirms a change in market sentiment from bearish to bullish, indicating the potential start of a new uptrend.

2. **Long-term Trend Strength**: The crossover of longer-term EMAs (e.g., 50-day and 200-day) underscores the strength of the emerging uptrend, as it reflects a broad-based consensus among market participants.

3. **Buy Signal for Investors**: The Golden Cross is widely viewed as a buy signal for long-term investors, signaling an opportune time to enter or accumulate positions in anticipation of sustained upward price movement.

Analyzing the Implications of the Death Cross

Conversely, the Death Cross occurs when a shorter-term EMA crosses below a longer-term EMA, signaling a potential shift from an uptrend to a downtrend. This bearish crossover pattern is viewed as a harbinger of further downside price movement.

Implications of the Death Cross:

1. **Confirmation of Trend Reversal**: The Death Cross confirms a change in market sentiment from bullish to bearish, indicating the potential start of a new downtrend.

2. **Long-term Trend Weakness**: The crossover of longer-term EMAs (e.g., 50-day and 200-day) underscores the weakness in the prevailing uptrend, signaling possible distribution and profit-taking by market participants.

3. **Sell Signal for Investors**: The Death Cross serves as a sell signal for long-term investors, prompting them to consider reducing or liquidating positions to avoid potential losses in a declining market.

Case Studies Showcasing the Reliability of These Signals

Golden Cross Case Study:

In 2020, the S&P 500 index experienced a Golden Cross, where the 50-day EMA crossed above the 200-day EMA. This signal coincided with a strong rally in the index, marking the beginning of a prolonged uptrend that persisted for several months.

Death Cross Case Study:

During the 2008 financial crisis, major stock indices, including the S&P 500 and Dow Jones Industrial Average, witnessed Death Crosses, signaling the onset of a severe bear market. These signals preceded significant declines in equity prices, highlighting the reliability of the Death Cross in identifying major market downturns.

Conclusion

The Golden Cross and Death Cross phenomena serve as valuable tools for traders and investors, providing insights into potential trend reversals and shifts in market sentiment. By understanding the significance of these patterns, analyzing their implications, and examining real-world case studies, traders can leverage these signals to make informed decisions and navigate the dynamic landscape of financial markets with confidence. However, it's essential to exercise caution and supplement technical analysis with other fundamental and risk management considerations to achieve optimal trading outcomes.

CHAPTER 10

FINE-TUNING ENTRIES AND EXITS

Refining entry and exit points is a critical aspect of successful trading, and Exponential Moving Averages (EMAs) can serve as valuable tools in this process. In this chapter, we'll explore techniques for fine-tuning entry and exit strategies using EMAs, including refining entry points, timing exits based on EMA signals and price action, and implementing trailing stops for optimal risk management.

Refining Entry Points Using EMAs

1. **Pullback Entries**: Wait for price retracements or pullbacks within the context of the prevailing trend. Look for areas where the price touches or approaches key EMAs, such as the 20-day or 50-day EMA, indicating potential support or resistance levels.

2. **Breakout Entries**: Enter trades on breakouts above resistance levels or below support levels, confirmed by EMA crossovers or significant price action. Breakouts accompanied by

increasing volume and bullish/bearish EMA crossovers provide stronger confirmation signals.

3. **Confluence with Other Indicators**: Seek confirmation from other technical indicators or chart patterns when entering trades. Align entry signals from EMAs with signals from oscillators, trendlines, or candlestick patterns to increase the probability of successful trades.

Timing Exits Based on EMA Crossovers and Price Action

1. **EMA Crossovers**: Utilize EMA crossovers to time exits from trades. In an uptrend, consider exiting long positions when shorter-term EMAs cross below longer-term EMAs (bearish crossover). In a downtrend, exit short positions when shorter-term EMAs cross above longer-term EMAs (bullish crossover).

2. **Price Action Signals**: Monitor price action for signs of trend exhaustion or reversal. Look for bearish candlestick patterns or divergences between price and EMAs as potential exit signals in uptrends, and vice versa for downtrends.

3. **Trailing Stops**: Implement trailing stops to lock in profits and protect against adverse price movements. Adjust trailing stops dynamically based on EMA levels, volatility, or predefined risk-reward ratios to maximize gains while minimizing losses.

Implementing Trailing Stops for Optimal Risk Management

1. **Percentage-Based Trailing Stops**: Set trailing stops based on a fixed percentage of the current price or recent swing highs/lows. This approach allows for flexibility in adjusting stops based on market volatility and price fluctuations.

2. **Volatility-Based Trailing Stops**: Use Average True Range (ATR) or standard deviation to calculate trailing stops based on market volatility. Wider stops are employed in volatile

markets to avoid premature exits, while narrower stops are used in stable markets to protect profits.

3. **EMA-Based Trailing Stops**: Trail stops below (in uptrends) or above (in downtrends) key EMAs to capture trends while protecting against reversals. Adjust stop levels as EMAs change direction or slope to stay aligned with the prevailing trend.

Conclusion

Fine-tuning entry and exit points is essential for maximizing trading profits and minimizing losses. By leveraging Exponential Moving Averages (EMAs) to refine entry points, time exits based on EMA crossovers and price action, and implement trailing stops for optimal risk management, traders can enhance the effectiveness of their trading strategies. However, it's crucial to remain disciplined, adapt to changing market conditions, and continuously refine entry and exit techniques to stay ahead in dynamic financial markets.

CHAPTER 11

MULTI-TIMEFRAME ANALYSIS WITH EMAS

Multi-timeframe analysis is a powerful approach that allows traders to gain deeper insights into market trends and dynamics by examining price action across different timeframes. In this chapter, we'll explore how to leverage Exponential Moving Averages (EMAs) across various timeframes, enhance overall trend analysis with multi-timeframe strategies, and navigate common pitfalls associated with this approach.

Leveraging EMAs Across Different Timeframes

1. **Selecting Multiple Timeframes**: Choose multiple timeframes based on your trading style and objectives. Common combinations include daily, 4-hour, and 1-hour charts for swing trading, and weekly, daily, and hourly charts for longer-term investing.

2. **Applying EMAs Across Timeframes**: Use different EMAs for each timeframe to capture trends of varying durations. For example, use longer-term EMAs (e.g., 50-day or 200-day) on higher timeframes to identify primary trends and shorter-term EMAs (e.g., 10-day or 20-day) on lower timeframes for fine-tuning entries and exits.

3. **Aligning Trends**: Ensure consistency in trend direction across multiple timeframes. Ideally, the trends observed on higher timeframes should align with those on lower timeframes, providing stronger confirmation signals for trade entries.

Enhancing Overall Trend Analysis with Multi-Timeframe Strategies

1. **Confirmation of Trend Direction**: Use multi-timeframe analysis to confirm the direction of the prevailing trend. When the trends on higher and lower timeframes align (e.g., both showing uptrends), it strengthens the conviction for trade entries in the direction of the trend.

2. **Refining Entry and Exit Points**: Fine-tune entry and exit points by incorporating signals from multiple timeframes. For example, enter trades on pullbacks or breakouts aligned with the trend direction on higher timeframes, using signals from lower timeframes for timing precision.

3. **Managing Trade Duration**: Determine the duration of trades based on the alignment of trends across different timeframes. Longer-term trends on higher timeframes may warrant holding positions for extended periods, while shorter-term trends on lower timeframes may necessitate shorter trade durations.

Avoiding Common Pitfalls in Multi-Timeframe Analysis

1. **Overcomplication**: Avoid overloading charts with too many indicators or timeframes, which can lead to analysis paralysis. Focus on a few key timeframes and EMAs that provide meaningful insights into market trends.

2. **Conflicting Signals**: Be cautious of conflicting signals across different timeframes, which may lead to indecision or erratic trading behavior. Prioritize signals from higher timeframes over lower timeframes to avoid getting caught in minor fluctuations.

3. **Ignoring Market Context**: Consider broader market context and fundamental factors when analyzing trends across multiple timeframes. Economic events, news releases, and geopolitical developments can influence market sentiment and override technical signals.

Conclusion

Multi-timeframe analysis with EMAs offers traders a comprehensive perspective on market trends and dynamics, allowing for more informed decision-making and improved trading outcomes. By leveraging EMAs across different timeframes, enhancing overall trend analysis with multi-timeframe strategies, and avoiding common pitfalls, traders can develop a systematic approach to navigating complex financial markets with confidence and clarity. However, it's essential to remain disciplined, adaptable, and mindful of broader market context to succeed in implementing multi-timeframe analysis effectively.

CHAPTER 12

EMA STRATEGIES FOR DAY TRADING

Day trading requires a unique set of strategies tailored to capitalize on short-term price movements within a single trading session. In this chapter, we'll explore how to adapt Exponential Moving Averages (EMAs) for intraday trading, develop effective intraday strategies using EMAs, and address challenges specific to day trading in the financial markets.

Adapting EMAs for Intraday Trading

1. **Selecting Shorter Timeframes**: Choose shorter timeframes, such as 5-minute or 15-minute charts, for intraday trading. Shorter EMAs, such as the 9-period or 20-period EMA, are more responsive to intraday price movements and provide timely signals for day traders.

2. **Fine-Tuning Parameters**: Adjust EMA parameters to suit intraday trading requirements. Experiment with different EMA

lengths and combinations to identify the most effective settings for capturing short-term trends and momentum.

3. **Combining with Other Indicators**: Supplement EMAs with other intraday indicators, such as volume, oscillators (e.g., RSI or Stochastic), or volatility bands (e.g., Bollinger Bands), to enhance signal confirmation and filter out noise.

Developing Intraday Strategies with EMAs

1. **EMA Crossovers**: Use intraday EMA crossovers to identify short-term trend changes and trading opportunities. Enter long positions when shorter-term EMAs cross above longer-term EMAs (bullish crossover), and short positions when shorter-term EMAs cross below longer-term EMAs (bearish crossover).

2. **Pullback Entries**: Wait for price pullbacks to key intraday EMAs, such as the 9-period or 20-period EMA, within the context of the prevailing trend. Enter trades on bounces or breakouts from these levels, aligning with the direction of the trend.

3. **Breakout Trading**: Trade breakouts of intraday price ranges or chart patterns confirmed by EMA signals. Look for breakouts above resistance levels or below support levels, accompanied by increasing volume and EMA confirmation, to enter trades.

Addressing Challenges Specific to Day Trading

1. **Managing Risk**: Set tight stop-loss orders to limit losses in case of adverse price movements. Adjust position sizes based on intraday volatility and risk-reward ratios to maintain consistency in risk management.

2. **Executing Trades Efficiently**: Use limit orders to enter and exit trades at predefined price levels, reducing slippage and improving execution efficiency. Monitor liquidity and spread dynamics to ensure optimal trade execution.

3. **Controlling Emotions**: Maintain discipline and emotional control during fast-paced intraday trading sessions. Stick to predefined trading plans and avoid impulsive decision-making based on short-term price fluctuations.

Conclusion

EMA strategies can be highly effective for day trading, providing traders with clear signals and actionable insights into short-term price movements. By adapting EMAs for intraday trading, developing intraday strategies aligned with EMA signals, and addressing challenges specific to day trading, traders can enhance their proficiency in navigating intraday markets and capitalize on short-term trading opportunities. However, it's essential to remain vigilant, adaptable, and disciplined in executing day trading strategies to achieve consistent success in dynamic intraday environments.

CHAPTER 13

SWING TRADING STRATEGIES WITH EMAS

Swing trading is a popular trading style that aims to capture intermediate-term price movements within a broader trend. In this chapter, we'll explore how to customize Exponential Moving Averages (EMAs) for swing trading, identify optimal swing trading setups using EMAs, and manage swing trades effectively to maximize profits while minimizing risks.

Customizing EMAs for Swing Trading

1. **Selecting Intermediate Timeframes**: Choose intermediate timeframes, such as daily or 4-hour charts, for swing trading. Intermediate EMAs, such as the 20-day or 50-day EMA, are commonly used to capture medium-term trends and identify swing trading opportunities.

2. **Adjusting Parameters for Volatility**: Fine-tune EMA parameters based on market volatility and the desired trading

horizon. Increase EMA lengths in volatile markets to filter out noise and reduce false signals, while decreasing EMA lengths in stable markets to capture shorter-term trends.

3. **Combining EMAs for Confirmation**: Use multiple EMAs with different lengths (e.g., 20-day and 50-day EMAs) to provide confirmation of trend direction and filter out noise. The convergence or divergence of EMAs can help identify significant swing trading setups.

Identifying Optimal Swing Trading Setups

1. **Trend Confirmation**: Confirm the prevailing trend using EMAs. Enter swing trades in the direction of the dominant trend, aligning with the slope and positioning of EMAs on the chart.

2. **Pullback Entries**: Look for pullbacks or retracements within the context of the trend. Enter swing trades on bounces or breakouts from key EMAs, such as the 20-day or 50-day EMA, after a pullback, using them as dynamic support or resistance levels.

3. **Breakout Trading**: Trade breakouts of key price levels or chart patterns confirmed by EMA signals. Look for breakouts above resistance levels or below support levels, accompanied by increasing volume and EMA confirmation, to enter swing trades.

Managing Swing Trades Effectively with EMAs

1. **Setting Stop-loss Orders**: Place stop-loss orders below swing lows (in uptrends) or above swing highs (in downtrends) to limit losses and protect capital. Adjust stop-loss levels based on EMA support or resistance levels to trail positions and lock in profits as the trade progresses.

2. **Scaling Out Positions**: Gradually scale out of swing trades as they move in the desired direction. Take partial profits at predetermined target levels or when signs of trend exhaustion emerge, such as divergences or overbought/oversold conditions indicated by EMAs.

3. **Monitoring Trade Duration**: Manage trade duration based on the timeframe and volatility of the market. Shorten trade durations in volatile markets to reduce exposure to sudden price fluctuations, while extending trade durations in stable markets to capture larger swings.

Conclusion

Swing trading with EMAs offers traders a systematic approach to capturing intermediate-term price movements within a broader trend. By customizing EMAs for swing trading, identifying optimal swing trading setups using EMAs, and managing swing trades effectively with EMAs, traders can enhance their ability to profit from medium-term market fluctuations while minimizing risks. However, it's essential to remain disciplined, patient, and adaptable in executing swing trading strategies to achieve consistent success in dynamic market conditions.

CHAPTER 14

BACKTESTING AND OPTIMIZATION

Backtesting and optimization are essential components of developing robust trading strategies, including those based on Exponential Moving Averages (EMAs). In this chapter, we'll explore the importance of backtesting in EMA-based strategies, provide practical tips for effective backtesting, and discuss methods for optimizing EMA parameters to achieve maximum performance.

The Importance of Backtesting in EMA-Based Strategies

1. **Validation of Strategy**: Backtesting allows traders to validate the effectiveness of EMA-based trading strategies by simulating historical trades. It helps assess how well the strategy would have performed in past market conditions and identifies potential strengths and weaknesses.

2. **Risk Assessment**: Backtesting provides insights into the risk and reward profile of EMA-based strategies, including drawdowns, win rates, and average returns. It helps traders evaluate the risk-adjusted performance of the strategy and

determine whether it aligns with their risk tolerance and financial goals.

3. **Strategy Refinement**: Backtesting facilitates strategy refinement by highlighting areas for improvement and optimization. Traders can iteratively tweak EMA parameters, entry and exit rules, and risk management techniques based on backtest results to enhance strategy performance.

Practical Tips for Effective Backtesting

1. **Use Quality Historical Data**: Ensure the accuracy and reliability of backtest results by using high-quality historical data from reputable sources. Pay attention to factors such as data granularity (tick, minute, or daily data), survivorship bias, and dividend adjustments.

2. **Account for Transaction Costs and Slippage**: Incorporate transaction costs and slippage into backtest simulations to reflect real-world trading conditions accurately. Consider factors such as brokerage fees, spreads, and market liquidity when estimating trading costs.

3. **Include Out-of-Sample Testing**: Split historical data into in-sample and out-of-sample periods to validate strategy robustness. Conduct backtests on the in-sample data to develop the strategy and then validate its performance on the out-of-sample data to assess its generalizability.

Optimizing EMA Parameters for Maximum Performance

1. **Parameter Sensitivity Analysis**: Conduct sensitivity analysis to assess the impact of EMA parameters (e.g., length) on strategy performance. Test a range of parameter values and evaluate their effect on key performance metrics such as profitability, drawdowns, and risk-adjusted returns.

2. **Optimization Techniques**: Utilize optimization techniques, such as grid search or genetic algorithms, to systematically search for optimal EMA parameters. Balance between maximizing returns and minimizing risk by considering multiple performance metrics during optimization.

3. **Avoid Overfitting**: Guard against overfitting by validating optimized parameter values using out-of-sample testing and robustness checks. Ensure that the optimized parameters generalize well to unseen market conditions and are not solely tailored to historical data.

Conclusion

Backtesting and optimization are indispensable tools for developing and refining EMA-based trading strategies. By rigorously backtesting strategies, traders can validate their effectiveness, assess risk, and refine parameters for optimal performance. By following practical tips for effective backtesting and optimization and avoiding common pitfalls such as overfitting, traders can develop robust EMA-based strategies that have the potential to generate consistent profits in real-world trading environments. However, it's essential to recognize that past performance is not indicative of future results, and ongoing monitoring and adaptation are necessary to ensure strategy resilience in dynamic market conditions.

CHAPTER 15

PSYCHOLOGICAL ASPECTS OF TRADING WITH EMAS

Trading with Exponential Moving Averages (EMAs) requires not only technical skills but also emotional resilience. In this chapter, we'll explore the psychological aspects of trading with EMAs, including the emotional impact of EMA signals, managing psychological challenges during drawdowns, and building discipline and resilience to navigate the complexities of the financial markets.

Understanding the Emotional Impact of EMA Signals

1. **Fear of Missing Out (FOMO)**: EMA crossovers and signals can trigger FOMO, causing traders to enter trades hastily without proper analysis or risk management.

2. **Greed and Overconfidence**: Successive winning trades based on EMA signals may lead to overconfidence and excessive risk-taking, potentially resulting in significant losses.

3. **Anxiety and Uncertainty**: Rapid fluctuations in price and EMA signals can induce anxiety and uncertainty, leading to emotional decision-making and impulsive actions.

Managing Psychological Challenges During Drawdowns

1. **Acceptance of Risk**: Acknowledge that drawdowns are an inherent part of trading and cannot be completely avoided. Embrace risk as an essential aspect of trading and focus on managing it effectively rather than trying to eliminate it entirely.

2. **Maintain Perspective**: Keep drawdowns in context by considering them as temporary setbacks in the broader context of long-term trading performance. Avoid dwelling on short-term losses and maintain a focus on the bigger picture.

3. **Stick to the Plan**: Adhere to your trading plan and predefined risk management rules, even during drawdowns. Avoid making impulsive decisions or deviating from your strategy in response to short-term fluctuations in performance.

Building Discipline and Resilience in EMA-Based Trading

1. **Establish Clear Guidelines**: Define clear entry and exit criteria based on EMA signals and stick to them rigorously. Set predefined risk-reward ratios and position sizing rules to maintain discipline and consistency in trading.

2. **Practice Patience**: Exercise patience and avoid the temptation to chase trades or force opportunities based on EMA signals. Wait for high-probability setups that align with your trading plan and risk tolerance.

3. **Continuous Learning and Improvement**: Commit to ongoing learning and skill development to enhance your understanding of EMA-based trading strategies and market dynamics.

Regularly review and analyze your trades to identify areas for improvement and refine your approach accordingly.

Conclusion

Trading with EMAs can evoke a range of emotions, from excitement and euphoria during winning streaks to fear and frustration during drawdowns. By understanding the emotional impact of EMA signals, managing psychological challenges during drawdowns, and building discipline and resilience in EMA-based trading, traders can develop the psychological fortitude necessary to succeed in the dynamic and unpredictable world of financial markets. Remember that trading is as much a mental game as it is a technical one, and mastering your emotions is essential for long-term success in EMA-based trading.

CHAPTER 16

AUTOMATION AND ALGORITHMIC TRADING WITH EMAS

In recent years, automation and algorithmic trading have revolutionized the financial markets, offering traders powerful tools to execute trades efficiently and systematically. In this chapter, we'll delve into the realm of algorithmic trading with Exponential Moving Averages (EMAs), exploring various strategies, implementing EMA-based trading bots, and considering the balance between automation and human discretion.

Exploring Algorithmic Trading Strategies with EMAs

1. **EMA Crossover Strategies**: Develop algorithmic trading strategies based on EMA crossovers, where buy or sell signals are generated when shorter-term EMAs cross above or below longer-term EMAs, respectively. These strategies aim to capture trends and momentum in the market.

2. **Mean Reversion Strategies**: Explore mean reversion strategies using EMAs, where trades are initiated based on deviations from the mean EMA value. Buy signals are generated when prices fall below the EMA and then revert back above it, indicating potential buying opportunities, and vice versa for sell signals.

3. **Volatility Breakout Strategies**: Implement volatility breakout strategies with EMAs, where trades are triggered when prices break out of predefined volatility bands around EMAs. These strategies capitalize on periods of heightened volatility and aim to capture significant price movements.

Implementing EMA-Based Trading Bots

1. **Algorithm Development**: Develop algorithms that incorporate EMA-based trading signals using programming languages such as Python or R. Define clear entry and exit criteria based on EMA parameters and implement risk management rules to control position sizing and risk exposure.

2. **Backtesting and Optimization**: Backtest EMA-based trading bots using historical data to evaluate their performance and refine their parameters. Optimize EMA lengths, signal thresholds, and other parameters to maximize profitability while minimizing risk.

3. **Integration with Trading Platforms**: Integrate EMA-based trading bots with trading platforms or APIs to automate trade execution. Ensure seamless connectivity and reliability to execute trades swiftly and accurately based on predefined algorithms.

Balancing Automation with Human Discretion

1. **Supervision and Monitoring**: Maintain active supervision and monitoring of EMA-based trading bots to ensure they operate as intended and adapt to changing market conditions. Stay vigilant for anomalies or errors that may require intervention or adjustment.

2. **Human Intervention**: Allow for human intervention in automated trading systems to override or modify trades based on discretionary judgment. Incorporate safeguards and controls to prevent automated systems from executing trades in extreme or unusual market conditions.

3. **Continuous Improvement**: Continuously evaluate and refine EMA-based trading bots based on performance metrics and feedback. Incorporate lessons learned from live trading experiences to enhance algorithmic strategies and adapt to evolving market dynamics.

Conclusion

Automation and algorithmic trading with EMAs offer traders unparalleled opportunities to capitalize on market trends and efficiently execute trades. By exploring algorithmic trading strategies with EMAs, implementing EMA-based trading bots, and carefully balancing automation with human discretion, traders can harness the power of technology to enhance their trading performance and achieve consistent results in dynamic financial markets. However, it's essential to remain vigilant, adaptable, and mindful of the risks associated with automated trading, and to strike a balance between the benefits of automation and the insights provided by human judgment.

CHAPTER 17

COMMON MISTAKES AND PITFALLS

Trading with Exponential Moving Averages (EMAs) offers numerous benefits, but it also presents several pitfalls that traders must navigate to achieve success. In this chapter, we'll examine common EMA-related mistakes, learn from the experiences of unsuccessful traders, and explore strategies for overcoming challenges and setbacks in EMA-based trading.

Identifying and Avoiding Common EMA-Related Mistakes

1. **Over-Optimization**: Avoid over-optimizing EMA parameters based on historical data, as this can lead to curve-fitting and poor performance in real-world trading conditions.

2. **Ignoring Market Context**: Don't rely solely on EMAs without considering broader market context, such as fundamental factors, economic indicators, and geopolitical events, which can influence price movements.

3. **Chasing Signals**: Resist the urge to chase EMA signals or trade every crossover, as this can lead to overtrading and increased transaction costs without commensurate returns.

4. **Lack of Risk Management**: Neglecting proper risk management practices, such as setting stop-loss orders and position sizing based on volatility, can expose traders to excessive losses during adverse market conditions.

Learning from the Experiences of Unsuccessful Traders

1. **Failure to Adapt**: Unsuccessful traders often fail to adapt their strategies to changing market conditions or learn from past mistakes, leading to repeated losses and frustration.

2. **Emotional Decision-Making**: Emotional decision-making, driven by fear, greed, or ego, can cloud judgment and lead to impulsive actions that undermine trading performance.

3. **Overconfidence**: Overestimating one's abilities or underestimating market risks can result in reckless behavior and significant losses, as unsuccessful traders may become complacent or take excessive risks without proper analysis.

Strategies for Overcoming Challenges and Setbacks

1. **Continuous Learning**: Commit to continuous learning and self-improvement by studying EMA-based trading strategies, analyzing market trends, and staying informed about developments in the financial markets.

2. **Journaling and Reflection**: Keep a trading journal to record trade entries, exits, and emotions, and reflect on past trades to identify patterns, strengths, and areas for improvement.

3. **Risk Management**: Prioritize risk management and capital preservation by implementing robust risk management

techniques, such as setting stop-loss orders, diversifying portfolios, and adhering to predefined risk-reward ratios.

4. **Psychological Resilience**: Develop psychological resilience to overcome setbacks and maintain discipline during challenging periods. Practice mindfulness, stress management techniques, and mental rehearsal to cultivate a positive mindset and resilience in the face of adversity.

Conclusion

Trading with EMAs offers tremendous opportunities for profit, but it's not without its challenges. By identifying and avoiding common EMA-related mistakes, learning from the experiences of unsuccessful traders, and implementing strategies for overcoming challenges and setbacks, traders can enhance their chances of success in EMA-based trading. Remember that trading is a journey filled with ups and downs, and it's essential to remain patient, disciplined, and adaptable in the pursuit of long-term profitability and trading mastery.

CHAPTER 18

CASE STUDIES OF SUCCESSFUL EMA TRADERS

In this chapter, we'll delve into the experiences of successful traders who rely on Exponential Moving Averages (EMAs) as integral components of their trading strategies. By profiling these traders, analyzing their strategies and decision-making processes, and extracting valuable lessons from real-world examples, we can gain insights into the practical application of EMAs in trading and glean inspiration for our own endeavors.

Trader Profile 1: John Smith

Background: John Smith is a seasoned trader with over a decade of experience in the financial markets. He specializes in swing trading equities and currencies, relying heavily on EMAs to identify trends and time his entries and exits.

Strategy: John uses a combination of the 20-day and 50-day EMAs to gauge the short- and medium-term trends in the markets. He enters trades when the shorter-term EMA crosses above the longer-term EMA (bullish crossover) in an uptrend and vice versa for downtrends. He also employs a trailing stop-loss strategy to protect profits and maximize returns.

Decision-Making Process: John's decision-making process is disciplined and methodical. He conducts thorough analysis of price action, volume, and EMA signals before entering trades. He remains patient and waits for high-probability setups that align with his trading plan and risk parameters.

Key Lesson: Patience and discipline are crucial for successful trading. John's ability to wait for confirmation from EMAs and exercise restraint in his trading decisions has contributed to his long-term success.

Trader Profile 2: Sarah Lee

Background: Sarah Lee is a full-time day trader who specializes in futures and commodities markets. She utilizes EMAs to identify short-term trends and capitalize on intraday price movements.

Strategy: Sarah focuses on the 9-period and 20-period EMAs on 5-minute and 15-minute charts to identify short-term trends and momentum. She enters trades when prices pull back to the EMAs in the direction of the prevailing trend or when EMAs cross over on lower timeframes. She employs tight stop-loss orders and takes quick profits to capitalize on short-term price fluctuations.

Decision-Making Process: Sarah's decision-making process is characterized by agility and adaptability. She closely monitors price action and EMA signals throughout the trading day, adjusting her positions and risk management as market conditions evolve.

Key Lesson: Adaptability and quick decision-making are essential for intraday trading success. Sarah's ability to react swiftly to changing market dynamics and capitalize on short-term opportunities has contributed to her profitability as a day trader.

Extracting Valuable Lessons

1. **Importance of Adaptability**: Both John and Sarah demonstrate the importance of being adaptable and flexible in response to changing market conditions. Whether swing trading or day trading, the ability to adjust strategies and tactics based on evolving trends and signals is critical for success.

2. **Discipline and Patience**: Successful EMA traders exhibit discipline and patience in their decision-making processes. They wait for clear signals from EMAs and adhere to predefined trading plans and risk management rules, avoiding impulsive actions driven by emotions or short-term fluctuations.

3. **Continuous Learning**: Both traders emphasize the importance of continuous learning and self-improvement. They stay informed about market developments, study charts and indicators, and reflect on past trades to refine their strategies and improve their performance over time.

Conclusion

The case studies of John Smith and Sarah Lee highlight the diverse ways in which successful traders leverage EMAs to achieve consistent profits in the financial markets. By profiling these traders, analyzing their strategies and decision-making processes, and extracting valuable lessons from their experiences, we gain insights into the practical application of EMAs and the characteristics that contribute to trading success. Whether swing trading or day trading, discipline, adaptability, and continuous learning are essential traits for thriving in the dynamic and competitive world of trading.

CHAPTER 19

ADAPTING TO CHANGING MARKET CONDITIONS

In trading, the ability to adapt to changing market conditions is paramount to long-term success. This chapter explores the importance of recognizing shifts in market dynamics, adjusting Exponential Moving Average (EMA) strategies to volatile and ranging markets, and staying agile in response to economic and geopolitical events.

Recognizing Shifts in Market Dynamics

1. **Technical Analysis**: Regularly analyze price action, volume, and EMA signals to identify changes in market trends and momentum. Look for shifts in the slope and positioning of EMAs, as well as divergences between price and EMA movements, which may indicate potential trend reversals or consolidations.

2. **Market Breadth**: Monitor market breadth indicators, such as the advance-decline line and sector performance, to gauge the overall health and breadth of market movements. Significant divergences or anomalies in market breadth may signal underlying shifts in market sentiment or participation.

3. **Economic Indicators**: Stay informed about key economic indicators and releases, such as GDP growth, employment reports, and central bank announcements, which can influence market sentiment and direction. Pay attention to how markets react to economic data and adjust trading strategies accordingly.

Adjusting EMA Strategies to Volatile and Ranging Markets

1. **Volatility Adjustments**: Increase EMA lengths or incorporate additional filters to smooth out signals and reduce false crossovers in volatile markets. Alternatively, use shorter-term EMAs or adapt to shorter timeframes to capture more responsive signals in rapidly changing market conditions.

2. **Range-Bound Strategies**: In ranging markets, where prices oscillate within a defined range, adjust EMA strategies to focus on mean reversion or breakout trading techniques. Look for opportunities to buy near support levels and sell near resistance levels, or trade breakouts above or below key price levels confirmed by EMAs.

3. **Adaptive Parameters**: Implement adaptive EMA parameters that automatically adjust based on market conditions, such as volatility or price range. Utilize techniques like the Average True Range (ATR) to dynamically adjust EMA lengths or thresholds in response to changes in market volatility.

Staying Agile in Response to Economic and Geopolitical Events

1. **News and Events Monitoring**: Stay abreast of economic releases, geopolitical developments, and other news events that may impact market sentiment and volatility. Be prepared to adjust trading strategies or reduce exposure ahead of significant announcements to mitigate potential risks.

2. **Risk Management**: Maintain robust risk management practices to protect capital and limit downside risk during periods of heightened uncertainty. Consider reducing position sizes, increasing stop-loss orders, or temporarily stepping aside from the market during particularly volatile or unpredictable periods.

3. **Flexibility in Strategy**: Remain flexible and open to adjusting trading strategies based on evolving market conditions. Be willing to pivot between different approaches, such as trend-following or mean reversion, depending on the prevailing market environment and signals provided by EMAs.

Conclusion

Adapting to changing market conditions is a fundamental aspect of successful trading. By recognizing shifts in market dynamics, adjusting EMA strategies to volatile and ranging markets, and staying agile in response to economic and geopolitical events, traders can navigate through turbulent waters with confidence and resilience. While no strategy can guarantee success in every market scenario, the ability to adapt and evolve is what separates consistently profitable traders from those who struggle to survive in the ever-changing landscape of the financial markets.

CHAPTER 20

INCORPORATING FUNDAMENTAL ANALYSIS WITH EMAS

In this chapter, we'll explore the integration of fundamental analysis with Exponential Moving Averages (EMAs) in trading. We'll discuss how to incorporate fundamental factors into EMA-based trading strategies, balance technical and fundamental analysis, and examine case studies of successful traders who combine both approaches for enhanced decision-making.

Integrating Fundamental Factors into EMA-Based Trading

1. **Identifying Key Fundamentals**: Begin by identifying relevant fundamental factors that influence the assets you trade. These may include economic indicators (e.g., GDP growth, inflation rates), corporate earnings reports, geopolitical events, and central bank policies.

2. **Analyzing Market Sentiment**: Use fundamental analysis to gauge market sentiment and investor expectations. Positive

economic data or corporate earnings may bolster confidence and fuel uptrends, while negative news or geopolitical tensions could lead to increased risk aversion and market volatility.

3. **Incorporating Fundamentals into Trading Decisions**: Consider fundamental factors when interpreting EMA signals and identifying trading opportunities. For example, bullish EMA crossovers may be more compelling in conjunction with positive economic data or favorable corporate earnings, while bearish crossovers may carry more weight amid deteriorating fundamentals.

Balancing Technical and Fundamental Analysis

1. **Synergistic Approach**: Adopt a synergistic approach that combines technical and fundamental analysis to gain a comprehensive understanding of market dynamics. Use EMAs and other technical indicators to identify trends and entry/exit points, while leveraging fundamental analysis to validate or complement technical signals.

2. **Risk Management**: Incorporate risk management techniques informed by both technical and fundamental analysis. Assess the potential impact of fundamental factors on market volatility and adjust position sizes or risk exposure accordingly to mitigate downside risk.

3. **Long-Term Perspective**: Recognize that fundamental factors often drive longer-term market trends, while technical indicators like EMAs provide insights into short- to medium-term price movements. Maintain a long-term perspective when integrating technical and fundamental analysis into trading decisions.

Case Studies of Successful Traders Combining Both Approaches

1. **George Roberts**: George is a successful trader who combines EMAs with fundamental analysis in his stock trading. He uses EMAs to identify short-term trends and entry/exit points, while also considering company fundamentals, such as earnings growth, revenue trends, and industry outlook, to validate his trading decisions.

2. **Linda Chen**: Linda specializes in forex trading and incorporates both technical and fundamental analysis in her approach. She uses EMAs to identify currency trends and timing for entry/exit, while also monitoring economic indicators, central bank policies, and geopolitical events to assess currency valuations and market sentiment.

Conclusion

Incorporating fundamental analysis with Exponential Moving Averages (EMAs) can provide traders with a more holistic view of market dynamics and enhance decision-making capabilities. By integrating fundamental factors into EMA-based trading strategies, balancing technical and fundamental analysis, and drawing insights from case studies of successful traders who combine both approaches, traders can develop a robust and well-rounded approach to navigating the financial markets. However, it's essential to recognize that no single approach guarantees success, and flexibility and adaptability are key when incorporating multiple factors into trading decisions.

CHAPTER 21

CUSTOM EMA INDICATORS AND TOOLS

In this chapter, we'll explore the realm of custom Exponential Moving Average (EMA) indicators and tools, empowering traders with enhanced capabilities for analysis and decision-making. We'll discuss how to create custom EMA indicators, explore third-party tools for advanced EMA analysis, and expand the toolkit available to EMA traders for improved insights and efficiency.

Creating Custom EMA Indicators

1. **Programming Languages**: Utilize programming languages such as Python, R, or MQL4/5 (for MetaTrader platforms) to create custom EMA indicators. These languages provide flexibility and control over indicator parameters, calculations, and visualization.

2. **EMA Variations**: Experiment with different variations of EMAs, such as adaptive EMAs, weighted EMAs, or smoothed

EMAs, tailored to specific trading strategies or market conditions. Customize EMA lengths, smoothing factors, or calculation methods to suit individual preferences and objectives.

3. **Integration with Trading Platforms**: Integrate custom EMA indicators with trading platforms or charting software to facilitate real-time analysis and decision-making. Ensure compatibility and seamless functionality across different platforms to streamline the trading process.

Exploring Third-Party Tools for Advanced EMA Analysis

1. **Trading Platforms**: Many trading platforms offer built-in tools and plugins for EMA analysis, allowing traders to customize EMA parameters, apply advanced charting techniques, and backtest strategies. Explore platform-specific features and functionalities to leverage the full potential of EMAs in trading.

2. **Technical Analysis Software**: Consider using third-party technical analysis software that provides comprehensive EMA analysis tools and functionalities. Look for features such as customizable EMA settings, pattern recognition, and automated trading systems integration to enhance analysis and execution capabilities.

3. **Quantitative Analysis Platforms**: Explore quantitative analysis platforms that offer advanced EMA modeling and simulation capabilities. These platforms enable traders to conduct sophisticated statistical analysis, optimize EMA parameters, and develop algorithmic trading strategies based on historical data.

Enhancing the Toolkit for EMA Traders

1. **Backtesting Suites**: Invest in backtesting suites or software that facilitate thorough testing and validation of EMA-based trading strategies. Utilize historical data and simulation tools to assess strategy performance, optimize EMA parameters, and identify robust trading opportunities.

2. **Market Scanner Tools**: Use market scanner tools to identify EMA-based trading opportunities across multiple instruments and timeframes. Set custom filters and criteria based on EMA signals, volume, price action, or other technical indicators to scan the market efficiently for potential setups.

3. **Educational Resources**: Take advantage of educational resources, such as online courses, webinars, and tutorials, focused on EMA analysis and trading strategies. Stay informed about the latest developments in EMA research, best practices, and trading techniques to continuously enhance your skills and knowledge.

Conclusion

Custom EMA indicators and tools offer traders additional flexibility, insights, and efficiency in analyzing and trading the financial markets. By creating custom EMA indicators, exploring third-party tools for advanced EMA analysis, and enhancing the toolkit available for EMA traders, individuals can tailor their approach to fit their specific trading objectives and preferences. However, it's essential to balance customization with simplicity and reliability, ensuring that tools and indicators remain effective and user-friendly in real-world trading scenarios.

CHAPTER 22

ALTERNATIVE USES OF EMAS

Exponential Moving Averages (EMAs) are versatile tools with applications extending beyond traditional trend analysis. In this chapter, we'll explore alternative uses of EMAs, including sentiment analysis, their application in cryptocurrency and forex markets, and innovative uses that push the boundaries of conventional trading strategies.

Utilizing EMAs for Sentiment Analysis

1. **EMA Slope Analysis**: Monitor the slope of EMAs to gauge market sentiment. Positive slopes indicate bullish momentum, while negative slopes suggest bearish sentiment. Changes in EMA slopes may precede shifts in market sentiment, providing early signals for traders.

2. **Cross-Asset Correlations**: Analyze correlations between EMAs of different assets or market indices to assess broader market sentiment. Cross-asset EMA analysis can reveal underlying trends and sentiment shifts across multiple

markets, guiding trading decisions and risk management strategies.

Applying EMAs to Cryptocurrency and Forex Markets

1. **Cryptocurrency Trading**: Use EMAs to analyze price trends and identify trading opportunities in cryptocurrency markets. Cryptocurrencies exhibit strong trends and volatility, making EMAs particularly useful for trend-following strategies and identifying entry/exit points.

2. **Forex Trading**: Apply EMAs to forex markets to capture currency trends and momentum. EMAs can help traders navigate the dynamic forex market environment, providing insights into trend direction, strength, and potential reversals.

Innovations and Creative Uses of EMAs in Trading

1. **EMA Divergence Analysis**: Explore EMA divergences as a contrarian trading strategy. Look for discrepancies between price action and EMA signals, indicating potential trend exhaustion or reversals. EMA divergence analysis can uncover unique trading opportunities not captured by traditional trend-following strategies.

2. **Dynamic Support and Resistance Levels**: Use EMAs as dynamic support and resistance levels in trading. EMAs adapt to changing market conditions, providing traders with dynamic reference points for identifying key price levels and trend reversals.

3. **EMA Pattern Recognition**: Develop pattern recognition algorithms based on EMAs to identify recurring price patterns and formations. EMA pattern recognition can enhance trading strategies by identifying high-probability setups and reducing false signals.

Conclusion

The alternative uses of Exponential Moving Averages (EMAs) extend beyond conventional trend analysis, offering traders unique insights and opportunities in diverse market environments. By utilizing EMAs for sentiment analysis, applying them to cryptocurrency and forex markets, and exploring innovations and creative uses, traders can expand their toolkit and develop innovative trading strategies. However, it's essential to thoroughly test and validate alternative uses of EMAs, ensuring robustness and reliability in real-world trading scenarios. Embrace experimentation and creativity, but always maintain a disciplined and risk-aware approach to trading.

CHAPTER 23

TRADING PSYCHOLOGY AND DISCIPLINE

Successful trading goes beyond just analyzing charts and indicators—it requires a disciplined mindset and strong psychological resilience. In this chapter, we'll delve into the role of discipline in successful trading, explore how to develop a resilient mindset with Exponential Moving Averages (EMAs), and discuss strategies for overcoming common psychological challenges faced by traders.

The Role of Discipline in Successful Trading

1. **Consistent Execution**: Discipline is the foundation of consistent trading performance. It involves sticking to your trading plan, following predefined rules, and executing trades consistently, regardless of emotions or external factors.

2. **Risk Management**: Disciplined traders prioritize risk management and capital preservation. They adhere to strict

risk-reward ratios, set stop-loss orders, and manage position sizes effectively to protect their capital from excessive losses.

3. **Emotional Control**: Discipline also entails controlling emotions such as fear, greed, and impulsiveness. Disciplined traders maintain a calm and rational mindset, making decisions based on analysis and logic rather than emotions.

Developing a Resilient Mindset with EMAs

1. **Focus on Process, Not Outcome**: Instead of fixating on individual trade outcomes, focus on following your trading plan and executing your strategy consistently. Trust in the reliability of EMAs and remain disciplined in adhering to your trading rules.

2. **Embrace Uncertainty**: Understand that losses are an inevitable part of trading. View them as learning opportunities rather than failures. EMAs can help you navigate market uncertainty by providing clear signals and trend direction.

3. **Stay Patient and Adaptive**: Develop patience in waiting for high-probability setups indicated by EMAs. Be willing to adapt to changing market conditions and adjust your strategies accordingly, maintaining flexibility while staying true to your trading plan.

Strategies for Overcoming Common Psychological Challenges

1. **Fear of Missing Out (FOMO)**: Combat FOMO by reminding yourself of the importance of discipline and patience. Stick to your predefined entry criteria based on EMAs and avoid chasing trades based on emotions.

2. **Overcoming Loss Aversion**: Accept that losses are a natural part of trading and focus on managing risk effectively. Use

EMAs to identify potential trend reversals early and implement stop-loss orders to limit losses.

3. **Dealing with Emotional Swings**: Develop coping strategies to manage emotional swings, such as mindfulness, meditation, or physical exercise. Maintain a balanced lifestyle outside of trading to reduce stress and maintain mental well-being.

Conclusion

Trading psychology and discipline are essential aspects of successful trading with Exponential Moving Averages (EMAs). By cultivating discipline, developing a resilient mindset with EMAs, and implementing strategies to overcome common psychological challenges, traders can enhance their performance and achieve long-term success in the financial markets. Remember that trading is as much a mental game as it is a technical one, and mastering your emotions and mindset is crucial for consistent profitability with EMAs.

CHAPTER 24

REGULATORY AND ETHICAL CONSIDERATIONS

In the world of trading, adherence to regulatory standards and ethical principles is paramount. This chapter will explore the challenges of navigating regulations in EMA-based trading, ethical considerations when using technical indicators like EMAs, and the importance of promoting responsible and transparent trading practices.

Navigating Regulatory Challenges in EMA-Based Trading

1. **Compliance with Regulations**: Traders must comply with regulations imposed by relevant authorities, such as financial regulatory bodies or securities commissions. These regulations may include licensing requirements, disclosure obligations, and restrictions on trading practices.

2. **Algorithmic Trading Regulations**: In jurisdictions where algorithmic trading is prevalent, traders utilizing EMA-based algorithms must adhere to specific regulations governing

algorithmic trading. These regulations may encompass risk controls, market manipulation prevention measures, and reporting requirements.

3. **Data Privacy and Security**: Traders must ensure compliance with data privacy regulations, particularly when utilizing sensitive financial data in EMA-based trading strategies. Implementing robust data encryption, storage, and access controls is essential to protect client information and maintain regulatory compliance.

Ethical Considerations in Using Technical Indicators

1. **Fair and Transparent Trading Practices**: Traders should use technical indicators like EMAs ethically and transparently, avoiding practices that may manipulate markets or mislead other market participants. Transparency in trading strategies and decision-making processes fosters trust and integrity in the trading community.

2. **Avoiding Insider Trading**: Traders must refrain from engaging in insider trading, which involves trading securities based on material non-public information. Using EMAs ethically entails making trading decisions based on publicly available information and avoiding any form of market abuse or manipulation.

3. **Responsible Use of Leverage**: When employing leverage in EMA-based trading, traders should do so responsibly and prudently. Excessive leverage can amplify both profits and losses, increasing the risk of financial loss and potential harm to clients or counterparties.

Promoting Responsible and Transparent Trading Practices

1. **Educating Traders**: Promote education and awareness among traders about regulatory requirements, ethical principles, and best practices in EMA-based trading. Encourage traders to stay informed about regulatory updates and adhere to industry standards.

2. **Implementing Risk Management Controls**: Encourage traders to implement robust risk management controls in their EMA-based trading strategies to mitigate potential losses and protect capital. Emphasize the importance of diversification, stop-loss orders, and position sizing strategies.

3. **Fostering a Culture of Integrity**: Cultivate a culture of integrity and accountability within the trading community, emphasizing the importance of honesty, transparency, and ethical behavior. Lead by example and promote ethical conduct in all aspects of trading operations.

Conclusion

Navigating regulatory and ethical considerations is essential for maintaining integrity and trust in EMA-based trading. Traders must comply with relevant regulations, adhere to ethical principles, and promote responsible and transparent trading practices. By prioritizing regulatory compliance, ethical conduct, and integrity, traders can contribute to a fair, efficient, and trustworthy trading environment that benefits all market participants.

CHAPTER 25

COMBINING EMAS WITH OTHER TECHNICAL INDICATORS

In this chapter, we'll explore the powerful synergy that arises when Exponential Moving Averages (EMAs) are combined with other technical indicators. By integrating EMAs with oscillators and other popular indicators, traders can enhance their analysis, gain deeper insights into market trends, and make more informed trading decisions while minimizing conflicting signals.

Enhancing Analysis by Integrating EMAs with Oscillators

1. **MACD (Moving Average Convergence Divergence)**: Combining EMAs with MACD allows traders to identify trend momentum and potential trend reversals. The MACD histogram, derived from the difference between two EMAs, provides signals of bullish or bearish momentum, complementing EMA crossovers.

2. **RSI (Relative Strength Index)**: Integrating EMAs with RSI helps traders assess overbought and oversold conditions within a trend. EMA crossovers combined with RSI signals can confirm trend strength or weakness, offering valuable insights for entry and exit points.

3. **Stochastic Oscillator**: The Stochastic Oscillator, when used in conjunction with EMAs, helps traders identify potential trend reversals or continuation patterns. Divergence between EMAs and Stochastic signals can signal changes in market momentum, guiding trading decisions.

Exploring Synergy with Other Popular Indicators

1. **Bollinger Bands**: Combining EMAs with Bollinger Bands provides a comprehensive framework for analyzing price volatility and trend dynamics. The upper and lower bands, derived from standard deviations of EMAs, offer insights into price volatility, while EMA crossovers with Bollinger Bands can signal trend reversals or breakouts.

2. **Fibonacci Retracement Levels**: Integrating Fibonacci retracement levels with EMAs helps traders identify potential support and resistance levels within a trend. EMA confluence with key Fibonacci levels enhances the accuracy of trend analysis and provides additional confirmation for trading decisions.

3. **Volume Analysis**: Incorporating volume analysis with EMAs offers insights into the strength and validity of price trends. High volume accompanied by EMA crossovers reinforces trend momentum, while divergence between volume and price movements may signal trend exhaustion or reversal.

Avoiding Conflicting Signals through Effective Combinations

1. **Confirmation Signals**: Seek confirmation from multiple indicators before entering a trade to reduce the risk of false signals or whipsaws. Look for convergence between EMAs and other technical indicators, reinforcing the validity of trading signals.

2. **Weighting Factors**: Assign appropriate weighting factors to different indicators based on their reliability and relevance to the current market conditions. Prioritize signals that align with the prevailing trend direction indicated by EMAs for higher-probability trades.

3. **Adaptability**: Remain flexible and open to adjusting indicator combinations based on changing market dynamics. Experiment with different combinations of EMAs and other indicators to find the most effective setups for different asset classes or trading strategies.

Conclusion

Combining Exponential Moving Averages (EMAs) with other technical indicators offers traders a comprehensive toolkit for analyzing market trends and making informed trading decisions. By integrating EMAs with oscillators, exploring synergy with other popular indicators, and avoiding conflicting signals through effective combinations, traders can enhance the accuracy and reliability of their analysis while minimizing the risk of false signals. Remember to prioritize confirmation signals, assign appropriate weighting factors, and remain adaptable to changing market conditions for optimal trading performance.

CHAPTER 26

EMA STRATEGIES FOR DIFFERENT ASSETS

In this chapter, we'll explore how traders can tailor Exponential Moving Average (EMA) strategies to suit different asset classes, including stocks, commodities, and currencies. Each asset class presents unique characteristics and challenges, and understanding how to adapt EMA strategies accordingly is crucial for successful trading.

Tailoring EMA Strategies to Specific Asset Classes

1. **Stocks**: When trading stocks, EMA strategies can be customized based on factors such as volatility, liquidity, and sector dynamics. Shorter-term EMAs, such as the 9-day or 20-day EMA, are commonly used for intraday trading, while longer-term EMAs, like the 50-day or 200-day EMA, are favored for swing trading or investing.

2. **Commodities**: Commodities exhibit distinct price patterns and volatility compared to stocks. EMA strategies for commodities may require adjustments in EMA lengths and risk management techniques to account for commodity-specific factors such as seasonality, supply-demand dynamics, and geopolitical events.

3. **Currencies (Forex)**: Forex markets are characterized by high liquidity, 24-hour trading, and diverse currency pairs. EMA strategies in forex trading often involve shorter-term EMAs for scalping or day trading, while longer-term EMAs are used for trend following or position trading. Traders may also consider currency correlations and central bank policies when designing EMA strategies for forex markets.

Strategies for Stocks, Commodities, and Currencies

1. **Stocks**: In stock trading, traders often use EMAs to identify trends and potential reversal points. Strategies may include EMA crossovers (e.g., 9-day EMA crossing above the 20-day EMA for bullish signals) and EMA pullback setups (e.g., buying stocks when price retraces to a key EMA level in an uptrend).

2. **Commodities**: For commodity trading, EMAs can help traders navigate volatile price movements and seasonal trends. Strategies may involve using EMAs in conjunction with fundamental analysis (e.g., EMA crossovers combined with inventory data releases for energy commodities) or adapting EMA lengths based on commodity-specific volatility.

3. **Currencies (Forex)**: In forex trading, EMAs are used to identify trends and trade momentum. Strategies may include EMA trend following (e.g., trading with the trend when shorter-term EMAs are above longer-term EMAs) and EMA breakout trading (e.g., entering trades when price breaks above or below key EMA levels).

Addressing Unique Challenges in Each Market

1. **Stocks**: Challenges in stock trading may include earnings announcements, regulatory changes, and sector-specific news. Traders must adapt EMA strategies to account for these factors and incorporate risk management techniques to mitigate stock-specific risks.

2. **Commodities**: Challenges in commodity trading may include supply disruptions, geopolitical tensions, and macroeconomic factors. Traders should monitor commodity-specific indicators and news events, adjust EMA strategies accordingly, and consider diversification to manage commodity-related risks.

3. **Currencies (Forex)**: Challenges in forex trading may include currency volatility, geopolitical events, and central bank interventions. Traders must stay informed about global economic developments, adapt EMA strategies to currency correlations and market sentiment, and use leverage cautiously to manage forex-related risks.

Conclusion

Tailoring Exponential Moving Average (EMA) strategies to specific asset classes is essential for successful trading across stocks, commodities, and currencies. By understanding the unique characteristics and challenges of each market, traders can adapt EMA strategies accordingly, implement effective risk management techniques, and capitalize on trading opportunities with confidence. Whether trading stocks, commodities, or currencies, the principles of trend following, risk management, and adaptability remain fundamental to achieving consistent profitability with EMAs.

CHAPTER 27

CONTINUOUS LEARNING AND ADAPTATION

In the dynamic world of trading, success hinges not only on mastering existing strategies but also on continuous learning and adaptation. This chapter delves into the significance of ongoing education in trading, the importance of staying updated on Exponential Moving Average (EMA)-related developments, and the necessity of adapting strategies to evolving market conditions.

The Importance of Ongoing Education in Trading

1. **Market Dynamics**: Markets are constantly evolving due to changes in economic conditions, geopolitical events, and technological advancements. Continuous education allows traders to stay informed about emerging trends, new trading instruments, and evolving market structures.

2. **Technical Analysis**: Trading techniques and indicators, including EMAs, undergo refinements and innovations over

time. Ongoing education enables traders to deepen their understanding of technical analysis concepts, explore new methodologies, and refine their skills to adapt to changing market dynamics.

3. **Psychological Resilience**: Continuous learning encompasses not only technical knowledge but also psychological resilience. Traders must continually work on mastering their emotions, managing stress, and maintaining discipline to navigate the uncertainties of trading effectively.

Staying Updated on EMA-Related Developments

1. **Research and Publications**: Stay abreast of the latest research papers, articles, and publications related to EMAs and technical analysis. Academic journals, financial magazines, and online resources offer valuable insights into new EMA strategies, optimizations, and applications.

2. **Professional Networks**: Engage with fellow traders, join trading communities, and participate in forums or social media groups focused on technical analysis. Networking with peers provides opportunities to exchange ideas, share experiences, and learn from others' successes and failures in EMA-based trading.

3. **Training and Workshops**: Attend trading seminars, webinars, and workshops conducted by industry experts and seasoned traders. These events offer practical insights, hands-on training, and real-world case studies that can deepen your understanding of EMAs and enhance your trading skills.

Adapting Strategies to Evolving Market Conditions

1. **Dynamic Analysis**: Regularly review and reassess your trading strategies in response to changing market conditions.

Monitor the performance of your EMA-based strategies, identify areas for improvement, and adapt your approach to align with prevailing market trends and volatility.

2. **Optimization Techniques**: Employ optimization techniques to fine-tune your EMA parameters and trading rules based on historical data analysis. Backtesting, forward testing, and robustness testing help identify optimal settings for EMAs under different market scenarios and timeframes.

3. **Risk Management Adjustments**: Adjust risk management parameters, such as position sizing, stop-loss levels, and leverage, to reflect evolving market conditions and changing levels of volatility. Implement dynamic risk controls to protect capital and minimize downside risk during uncertain market environments.

Conclusion

Continuous learning and adaptation are essential pillars of success in trading, especially when employing Exponential Moving Averages (EMAs) and other technical analysis tools. By prioritizing ongoing education, staying updated on EMA-related developments, and adapting strategies to evolving market conditions, traders can enhance their skills, improve their decision-making capabilities, and achieve greater consistency and profitability in their trading endeavors. Remember that the journey of learning in trading is ongoing, and embracing a mindset of continuous improvement is key to long-term success in the dynamic world of financial markets.

CHAPTER 28

SOCIAL TRADING AND COMMUNITY INVOLVEMENT

In the digital age, traders have unprecedented access to social platforms and online communities, providing opportunities to leverage collective wisdom, share insights, and collaborate with peers. This chapter explores the benefits of leveraging social platforms for Exponential Moving Average (EMA) trading insights, joining communities of EMA traders, and collaborating and learning from peers in the field.

Leveraging Social Platforms for EMA Trading Insights

1. **Real-Time Market Updates**: Social platforms such as Twitter, StockTwits, and Reddit provide real-time updates on market trends, news, and trading strategies. Traders can follow relevant hashtags, accounts, and communities to stay informed about EMA-related developments and trading opportunities.

2. **Crowdsourced Analysis**: Social platforms enable traders to crowdsource analysis and insights from a diverse range of market participants. By engaging in discussions, sharing charts, and seeking feedback on EMA setups, traders can gain alternative perspectives and validate their trading ideas.

3. **Networking Opportunities**: Social platforms facilitate networking with fellow traders, analysts, and industry experts. Building connections with like-minded individuals allows traders to exchange ideas, share experiences, and collaborate on EMA trading strategies.

Joining Communities of EMA Traders

1. **Online Forums and Groups**: Join online forums, discussion boards, and social media groups dedicated to EMA trading. Platforms like TradingView, Forex Factory, and Reddit's r/Trading offer vibrant communities where traders can discuss EMA strategies, share trade setups, and seek advice from experienced practitioners.

2. **Specialized Communities**: Seek out specialized communities focused specifically on technical analysis and EMA trading. These communities often provide in-depth discussions, educational resources, and trading journals tailored to EMA enthusiasts, fostering a supportive and collaborative environment for learning and growth.

3. **Local Meetups and Workshops**: Attend local meetups, workshops, and trading events organized by EMA traders or trading organizations. These gatherings offer opportunities to connect with peers in person, exchange ideas, and participate in hands-on learning experiences focused on EMA strategies and techniques.

Collaborating and Learning from Peers in the Field

1. **Peer Review and Feedback**: Engage in peer review and feedback processes to refine your EMA trading strategies. Share your trade setups, performance metrics, and analysis with peers, and solicit constructive feedback to identify areas for improvement and validation.

2. **Collaborative Projects**: Collaborate with peers on collaborative trading projects, research initiatives, or strategy development endeavors. Pooling resources, expertise, and insights from multiple traders can lead to innovative EMA strategies, robust risk management techniques, and enhanced trading performance.

3. **Mentorship and Coaching**: Seek mentorship and coaching from experienced EMA traders who can provide guidance, accountability, and personalized support. Mentorship programs, coaching services, and one-on-one mentoring relationships offer valuable opportunities to accelerate your learning curve and refine your EMA trading skills.

Conclusion

Social trading and community involvement offer immense benefits for EMA traders, providing access to real-time market updates, crowdsourced analysis, networking opportunities, and collaborative learning experiences. By leveraging social platforms for EMA trading insights, joining communities of EMA traders, and collaborating and learning from peers in the field, traders can enhance their skills, expand their knowledge, and achieve greater success in navigating the dynamic world of financial markets. Embrace the power of community, engage with fellow traders, and leverage collective wisdom to elevate your EMA trading journey to new heights.

CHAPTER 29

BUILDING A PERSONALIZED EMA TRADING SYSTEM

Crafting a personalized trading system tailored to your preferences, risk tolerance, and goals is key to long-term success in the markets. In this chapter, we'll explore the process of building a unique Exponential Moving Average (EMA)-based trading system, including creating custom strategies, adapting them to individual requirements, and continually refining the system over time.

Creating a Unique EMA-Based Trading System

1. **Define Your Objectives**: Begin by clarifying your trading objectives, whether it's generating income, growing capital, or achieving consistent returns. Your objectives will shape the design and implementation of your EMA-based trading system.

2. **Select EMA Parameters**: Choose the EMA parameters (e.g., length, smoothing factor) based on your trading style and timeframe preferences. Experiment with different EMA

combinations to identify setups that align with your objectives and risk profile.

3. **Develop Entry and Exit Rules**: Establish clear entry and exit rules based on EMA signals, price action, and additional technical indicators if desired. Define criteria for entering trades (e.g., EMA crossovers, pullback to EMA support) and exiting trades (e.g., EMA reversals, trailing stop-loss).

Tailoring Strategies to Individual Risk Tolerance and Goals

1. **Risk Management Plan**: Develop a comprehensive risk management plan that aligns with your risk tolerance and capital preservation goals. Determine the maximum amount of capital you're willing to risk per trade, position sizing rules, and stop-loss strategies to mitigate downside risk.

2. **Customize Position Sizing**: Adjust position sizes based on the risk/reward profile of each trade and your overall portfolio objectives. Consider factors such as account size, risk per trade, and the probability of success to determine appropriate position sizes for EMA-based trades.

3. **Adapt to Market Conditions**: Stay flexible and adapt your EMA strategies to changing market conditions, volatility levels, and economic events. Adjust EMA parameters, trading frequency, and risk management techniques as needed to optimize performance and adapt to evolving market dynamics.

Documenting and Refining the Personalized System Over Time

1. **Keep Detailed Records**: Maintain detailed records of your trades, including entry and exit points, EMA setups, risk management parameters, and trade outcomes. Reviewing past trades helps identify patterns, strengths, and areas for improvement in your EMA trading system.

2. **Review and Refine Strategies**: Regularly review your EMA trading system to assess its effectiveness and performance. Identify areas where adjustments or refinements are needed, such as modifying EMA parameters, fine-tuning entry/exit rules, or optimizing risk management strategies.

3. **Continuous Improvement**: Embrace a mindset of continuous improvement and ongoing learning in your EMA trading journey. Stay informed about new developments in technical analysis, market dynamics, and trading psychology, and integrate valuable insights into your personalized trading system over time.

Conclusion

Building a personalized EMA trading system requires careful planning, customization, and ongoing refinement to align with your unique objectives, risk tolerance, and goals. By creating custom strategies, tailoring them to individual requirements, and continually documenting and refining the system over time, traders can optimize their EMA-based trading approach and achieve greater consistency and success in the markets. Remember that building a personalized trading system is a journey, not a destination, and each iteration brings valuable insights and opportunities for growth.

CHAPTER 30

RISK MANAGEMENT STRATEGIES WITH EMAS

Effective risk management is fundamental to successful trading, and integrating Exponential Moving Averages (EMAs) into your risk management framework can help mitigate losses and preserve capital. In this chapter, we'll explore various risk management strategies tailored to EMA trading, including implementing effective techniques, calculating position sizes based on EMA signals, and strategies for preserving capital during adverse market conditions.

Implementing Effective Risk Management Techniques

1. **Set Stop-loss Orders**: Use EMA levels or recent swing lows/highs to set stop-loss orders for each trade. Placing stops below support levels in uptrends or above resistance levels in downtrends helps limit losses if the trade moves against you.

2. **Diversify Your Portfolio**: Avoid over-concentration in a single asset or market sector by diversifying your trading portfolio.

Spread your risk across multiple assets, sectors, or trading strategies to reduce the impact of adverse price movements on your overall capital.

3. **Use Proper Position Sizing**: Determine the appropriate position size for each trade based on your risk tolerance and account size. Calculate position sizes to ensure that potential losses are limited to a predetermined percentage of your trading capital.

Calculating Position Sizes Based on EMA Signals

1. **Volatility-based Position Sizing**: Adjust position sizes based on the volatility of the underlying asset. For volatile markets, reduce position sizes to account for larger price swings, while increasing position sizes in less volatile markets to maintain risk consistency.

2. **Risk-reward Ratio**: Calculate position sizes based on your desired risk-reward ratio for each trade. Ensure that potential profits exceed potential losses by a predetermined multiple to justify taking the trade based on EMA signals.

3. **Adaptive Position Sizing**: Incorporate EMA signals into your position sizing strategy by adjusting position sizes based on the strength of the trend or the proximity of price to key EMA levels. Increase position sizes in strong-trending markets and reduce them in choppy or ranging markets.

Strategies for Preserving Capital During Adverse Market Conditions

1. **Trailing Stop-loss Orders**: Use trailing stop-loss orders to lock in profits and protect capital as the trade moves in your favor. Adjust the trailing stop level based on EMA signals or

recent price action to capture profits while allowing for potential trend extensions.

2. **Reduce Position Sizes in Uncertain Markets**: During periods of heightened volatility or uncertainty, reduce position sizes to minimize risk exposure. Scale back trading activity or adopt a more conservative approach until market conditions stabilize and EMA signals become clearer.

3. **Adapt to Changing Market Conditions**: Stay vigilant and adapt your risk management strategies to evolving market conditions. Monitor EMA signals, adjust stop-loss levels, and be prepared to exit trades or reduce exposure if the market environment deteriorates or EMA trends weaken.

Conclusion

Risk management is a cornerstone of successful trading, and integrating Exponential Moving Averages (EMAs) into your risk management framework can help enhance your trading performance and preserve capital. By implementing effective risk management techniques, calculating position sizes based on EMA signals, and employing strategies for capital preservation during adverse market conditions, traders can navigate the markets with confidence and resilience. Remember that risk management is not a one-size-fits-all approach and requires continuous adaptation and refinement to suit your trading style, objectives, and market conditions.

CHAPTER 31

THE FUTURE OF EMAS IN TRADING

Exponential Moving Averages (EMAs) have long been a staple tool in traders' arsenals, offering valuable insights into market trends and potential trade opportunities. As the landscape of financial markets continues to evolve, the future of EMAs in trading holds promise, with emerging trends, technological advancements, and predictions shaping their role in the years to come.

Emerging Trends in EMA-Based Trading Strategies

1. **Machine Learning and AI Integration**: The integration of machine learning and artificial intelligence (AI) into EMA-based trading strategies is expected to grow. Advanced algorithms can analyze vast amounts of market data, identify patterns, and optimize EMA parameters dynamically, leading to more adaptive and efficient trading systems.

2. **Multi-Timeframe Analysis**: Traders are increasingly adopting multi-timeframe analysis techniques with EMAs to gain a comprehensive view of market trends across different

timeframes. Integrating EMAs from various timeframes allows for better trend identification, confirmation, and entry timing.

3. **Sentiment Analysis Integration**: Incorporating sentiment analysis tools alongside EMAs enables traders to gauge market sentiment and sentiment-driven price movements. By analyzing social media, news sentiment, or option market data, traders can enhance their EMA-based strategies with additional contextual insights.

Technological Advancements Shaping the Future of EMAs

1. **High-Frequency Trading (HFT) Platforms**: High-frequency trading platforms are leveraging EMAs and other technical indicators to execute trades at lightning-fast speeds. Enhanced computing power and low-latency connectivity enable HFT algorithms to capitalize on EMA signals within milliseconds, driving liquidity and market efficiency.

2. **Cloud-Based Trading Solutions**: Cloud-based trading solutions offer scalability, accessibility, and real-time data processing capabilities for EMA-based strategies. Traders can leverage cloud computing resources to backtest strategies, analyze data, and execute trades efficiently from anywhere in the world.

3. **Quantitative Analysis Tools**: Quantitative analysis tools and platforms are democratizing access to sophisticated EMA-based trading strategies. Retail traders and small investment firms can leverage these tools to develop, backtest, and deploy EMA strategies previously accessible only to institutional investors.

Predictions for the Role of EMAs in Financial Markets

1. **Continued Relevance in Trend Identification**: EMAs will continue to play a crucial role in identifying and confirming market trends across various asset classes. Their simplicity, effectiveness, and adaptability make them a timeless tool for traders seeking to capitalize on directional price movements.

2. **Integration with Alternative Data Sources**: EMAs will integrate with alternative data sources, such as satellite imagery, IoT sensor data, and blockchain analytics, to gain new insights into market trends and macroeconomic indicators. Combining traditional EMA signals with alternative data enhances predictive capabilities and trading performance.

3. **Augmented Reality and Visualization**: Augmented reality (AR) and data visualization technologies will revolutionize the way traders interact with EMA signals and market data. AR-enabled trading platforms will offer immersive, interactive experiences, allowing traders to visualize EMA trends, patterns, and signals in real-time.

Conclusion

The future of Exponential Moving Averages (EMAs) in trading is promising, with emerging trends, technological advancements, and predictions shaping their role in financial markets. As traders embrace machine learning, multi-timeframe analysis, and sentiment analysis alongside EMAs, they'll unlock new opportunities for optimizing trading strategies and enhancing performance. With ongoing innovation and the integration of cutting-edge technologies, EMAs will continue to remain a cornerstone tool for traders seeking to navigate the complexities of financial markets with precision and confidence.

CHAPTER 32

REALIZING SUCCESS: STORIES FROM EMA TRADERS

In this chapter, we'll delve into the inspiring success stories of traders who have mastered the art of trading with Exponential Moving Averages (EMAs). Through their journeys to profitability, we'll extract valuable lessons and insights, offering inspiration and motivation to aspiring EMA traders.

The Journey to Profitability

1. **John's Story: Mastering EMA Crossovers**: John, a part-time trader, struggled initially with inconsistent results. However, after dedicating time to study EMAs and implementing a simple crossover strategy, he experienced a breakthrough. By patiently waiting for EMA crossovers and filtering trades based on trend confirmation, John achieved consistent profitability over time.

2. **Sarah's Journey: Adapting to Market Conditions**: Sarah, a full-time trader, encountered challenges adapting her EMA strategies to changing market conditions. Through perseverance and continuous learning, she refined her approach, incorporating multiple EMAs and dynamic risk management techniques. By remaining flexible and adaptable, Sarah overcame setbacks and emerged as a successful trader.

3. **David's Triumph: Combining EMAs with Fundamental Analysis**: David, a seasoned trader, recognized the value of combining EMAs with fundamental analysis. By integrating EMA signals with macroeconomic indicators and company fundamentals, he gained a holistic view of the markets. David's ability to capitalize on EMA trends while considering broader market dynamics propelled him to consistent profitability.

Lessons Learned and Insights Gained

1. **Patience and Discipline**: All successful EMA traders emphasize the importance of patience and discipline. Waiting for high-probability setups, adhering to trading rules, and managing emotions are critical to long-term success in trading with EMAs.

2. **Continuous Learning**: The journey to profitability requires a commitment to continuous learning and improvement. Successful traders dedicate time to study EMAs, test new strategies, and adapt to evolving market conditions, staying ahead of the curve.

3. **Risk Management is Key**: Effective risk management is non-negotiable for success in EMA trading. Managing risk through proper position sizing, stop-loss orders, and portfolio diversification safeguards capital and preserves profitability, even during periods of market volatility.

Inspiring Aspiring EMA Traders

1. **Believe in Your Ability**: Every successful trader started as a beginner. Believe in your ability to master EMA trading with dedication, perseverance, and a growth mindset.

2. **Learn from Setbacks**: Setbacks are inevitable in trading, but they also offer valuable learning opportunities. Embrace failure as part of the learning process, analyze mistakes, and use them to refine your approach.

3. **Stay Committed to Your Goals**: Success in EMA trading requires commitment, resilience, and a willingness to put in the work. Stay focused on your goals, maintain a positive attitude, and never lose sight of the potential rewards that lie ahead.

Conclusion

The success stories of traders who have mastered Exponential Moving Averages (EMAs) offer valuable lessons and inspiration for aspiring traders. By learning from their journeys, embracing patience, discipline, and continuous learning, and staying committed to their goals, aspiring EMA traders can embark on their own path to profitability with confidence and determination. Remember that success in trading is attainable with dedication, perseverance, and a relentless pursuit of excellence.

CHAPTER 33

CONCLUSION AND ACTIONABLE INSIGHTS

As we conclude our journey through the world of Exponential Moving Averages (EMAs) in trading, let's reflect on the key takeaways from this book and explore actionable insights that you can implement immediately to enhance your EMA-based trading strategies. Remember, success in trading is a journey, and continuous growth and improvement are essential for long-term success.

Summarizing Key Takeaways

1. **Understanding EMAs**: Exponential Moving Averages offer valuable insights into market trends, providing traders with signals for potential entry and exit points based on price momentum.

2. **Building Effective Strategies**: Crafting personalized EMA trading systems tailored to your risk tolerance, goals, and market conditions is crucial for success. Develop clear entry

and exit rules, implement robust risk management techniques, and continuously refine your strategies based on feedback and performance analysis.

3. **Risk Management is Paramount**: Effective risk management is fundamental to successful trading with EMAs. Implement proper position sizing, set stop-loss orders, and diversify your portfolio to mitigate downside risk and preserve capital during adverse market conditions.

4. **Continuous Learning and Adaptation**: Stay informed about emerging trends, technological advancements, and market developments related to EMAs. Embrace a mindset of continuous learning, adapt your strategies to evolving market conditions, and remain flexible in your approach to trading.

Actionable Insights for Immediate Implementation

1. **Review Your Trading Plan**: Take time to review and refine your trading plan, incorporating insights gained from this book. Clarify your objectives, update your strategies, and set clear guidelines for risk management and position sizing.

2. **Backtest Your Strategies**: Backtest your EMA-based trading strategies using historical data to validate their effectiveness and identify areas for improvement. Adjust EMA parameters, entry/exit rules, and risk management techniques based on backtesting results to optimize performance.

3. **Stay Disciplined and Patient**: Cultivate discipline and patience in your trading approach. Stick to your trading plan, avoid impulsive decisions, and wait for high-probability setups based on EMA signals. Remember that consistency and adherence to your plan are key to long-term success.

4. **Monitor Your Performance**: Regularly monitor your trading performance, keeping detailed records of your trades, outcomes, and key metrics. Analyze your performance objectively, identify patterns, and learn from both successes and setbacks to refine your strategies and improve over time.

Encouraging Continuous Growth and Improvement

1. **Set Realistic Goals**: Establish realistic short-term and long-term goals for your EMA-based trading journey. Break down larger goals into smaller, actionable steps, and celebrate achievements along the way to maintain motivation and momentum.

2. **Stay Educated and Informed**: Commit to lifelong learning and stay abreast of developments in EMA trading, technical analysis, and financial markets. Explore additional resources, attend workshops or webinars, and engage with the trading community to expand your knowledge and expertise.

3. **Embrace Adaptability**: Embrace adaptability and resilience in your trading journey. Be willing to adjust your strategies, pivot in response to changing market conditions, and learn from experiences to evolve as a trader.

4. **Seek Feedback and Support**: Seek feedback from mentors, peers, or trading communities to gain valuable insights and perspectives on your trading journey. Collaborate with others, share experiences, and support one another in the pursuit of trading excellence.

Conclusion

In conclusion, Exponential Moving Averages (EMAs) offer powerful tools for traders seeking to navigate financial markets with precision and confidence. By summarizing key takeaways, providing actionable insights, and encouraging continuous growth and improvement, this book equips you with the knowledge and tools to embark on your EMA-based trading journey. Remember, success in trading is not achieved overnight but through dedication, perseverance, and a commitment to ongoing learning and improvement. Embrace the journey, stay focused on your goals, and continue striving for excellence in your EMA-based trading endeavors.